THE TEACHING OF CLASSICAL BALLET

COMMON FAULTS IN YOUNG DANCERS AND THEIR TRAINING

by

JOAN LAWSON

Second edition

WITH 160 PHOTOGRAPHS

ADAM & CHARLES BLACK · LONDON
THEATRE ARTS BOOKS · NEW YORK

SECOND EDITION 1983

FIRST PUBLISHED 1973

BY A & C BLACK (PUBLISHERS) LIMITED

35 BEDFORD ROW, LONDON WC1R 4JH

PUBLISHED SIMULTANEOUSLY IN THE USA
BY THEATRE ARTS BOOKS, 153 WAVERLY PLACE,
NEW YORK, NY 10014

UK ISBN 0 7136-2300-4

US ISBN 0-87830-583-1

© 1983, 1973 JOAN LAWSON

Lawson, Joan, *1906*–
    The teaching of classical ballet.—2nd ed.
    1. Ballet—Study and teaching—Handbooks,
    manuals, etc.
    I. Title
    792.8′2′07   GV1788
    ISBN 0-7136-2300-4

PRINTED IN GREAT BRITAIN BY
BAS PRINTERS LIMITED,
OVER WALLOP, HAMPSHIRE

LORETTE WILMOT LIBRARY
Nazareth College of Rochester

Rochester City Ballet

THE TEACHING OF CLASSICAL BALLET

CONTENTS

ACKNOWLEDGEMENTS

THIS BOOK was written and compiled after studying various methods of teaching classical dance to boys and girls, and discussing the faults which arise because teachers do not always take into account the way each child grows. I am particularly indebted to Dame Ninette de Valois for her constant encouragement of my research; to the great teacher Agrippina Jakovlevna Vaganova and the Staff of the Vaganova Choregraphic School in Leningrad; to Sophie Nikholaevna Golovkina and the Staff of the Moscow Choregraphic Academy; Natalia Dudinskaya and Konstantin Sergeyev of the Kirov Ballet; to Asaf Messerer and Irina Tikhomirnova of the Bolshoi Ballet. But my deepest gratitude goes to my colleagues at the Royal Ballet School for their help, criticism and adjustments to the technical details namely: Barbara Fewster, our principal for much valuable advice, and permission to use the children of the Royal Ballet School as models for the photos, Pamela May, Julia Farron and Valerie Adams, director of our Teacher Training Course; to Pauline Wadsworth for her care and thought in helping to solve problems with the younger classes and with Sara Neil, for helping to pose the photographs; to Professor Tanner of The Institute of Child Health for his most valuable contribution to my knowledge; to Alan Hooper of the Royal Academy of Dancing for much help in preparing the material; to Arthur Carter of the White Lodge academic staff for his enthusiasm and patience when taking the photographs; and finally to the children of Forms 1, 2 and 3 for their co-operation through many long sessions when they would much rather have been dancing.

I am deeply indebted to the late Professor Wiles of Middlesex Hospital for his advice and research on this subject.

Since this book was first published in 1972, many professional dancers have started a new career as teachers. Amongst them are several male teachers who have asked me to help them teach girls to dance *sur les pointes*. Thus at their specific request I have added a new chapter on training for *pointe* work, hoping it will answer some of their problems. I must now thank Ross MacGibbon of the Royal Ballet for taking the set of photographs illustrating this chapter, and Alan Hooper, director of the Royal Academy of Dancing, for allowing me to use the first-, second- and third-year scholars as models. In turn I must thank them all for giving their time and energy after lessons were finished.

Of the scholars who modelled the photographs in the first edition, the following all went into one or other of the Royal Ballets: Mark Welford, Matthew Hawkins, Andrew Ward, Siobhan Stanley and Chinca Williams. In addition, Lucy Bethune went to Rambert, Beth Keeble and Ashley Wheater to Festival Ballet (the latter is now with Australian Ballet), and all the others are now working in one of the European companies.

JOAN LAWSON

INTRODUCTION

THIS BOOK is an attempt to help teachers and those wishing to become teachers how to eliminate the common faults often found amongst both amateur and aspiring professional children studying Classical Dance. These faults are usually seen in growing girls and boys and can arise in many ways. The most outstanding are as follows:—

1. INCORRECT STANCE which can result in an over-arched back, over-turned feet, and loss of flexibility throughout the torso, head and arms because of tension and lack of stability in the supporting leg.

2. FAILURE TO UNDERSTAND THE CORRECT TILT OF THE PELVIS, i.e. the hinge-like movement of the torso and hip-joint, and the need to raise the weight firmly upwards away from the waist line, leading to a loss of the full extension of the legs and torso.

3. INCORRECT RISE TO THE *demi-pointe*, leading to the sickling of the foot and the loss of the straight line of the legs.

4. INCORRECT TRANSFER OF WEIGHT and proper use of the supporting leg, together with the failure of the foot to use the floor as a spring board and firm base for the dance.

5. BAD PLACING of the hand on the barre, poor use of the head and the focussing of the eyes as the child grows.

6. IGNORANCE OF THE ESSENTIAL DIFFERENCES to be made between the teaching of girls and boys.

7. FAILURE consistently to use the conventions of classical dance during the first years of training.

N.B. Positions of the arms are given according to the system adopted by the Royal Academy of Dancing.

I

THE IMPORTANCE OF STANCE

T HE most important principle to establish during the first lessons in classical dance is correct stance. If it is not clearly understood and practised as the first requisite for every boy and girl hoping for a professional career, they will ultimately suffer in some way or another. Even as amateurs, perhaps aiming to excel at some sport or have a career in physical education, or as coach to athletes, they will have problems through not understanding fully the proper alignments of all the bones of the body, their relationship to each other and to the centre line of balance which runs from the crown of the head to a point just over and between the two insteps. No matter how slight the discrepancy, it will affect the total carriage of the body in some way as it moves through steps, poses, runs and jumps.

It is not easy to teach stance to growing children and ensure that each of them can maintain this new upright classical stance throughout one exercise, particularly if growth is fast. The strain resulting from having to move the extra weight of bone is not usually accompanied by the strengthening of lengthening muscles (see Chapter 7). Thus children's ability to control their movements at all times is limited. Even those who grow more slowly and whose problems are not great, still often strain in performance. This is probably because they instinctively feel and can usually recognise when the movement looks right and are determined to keep it so, but fail to realise that the muscles do not have the same degree of strength. Nevertheless both types of children must be helped in the same class because fast growers may as suddenly stop growing, and those children then learn to stabilise themselves. On the other hand the gradual growers can put on sudden spurts, particularly girls. But it is not usual. Teachers must therefore stress the correct holding of the body as the first task in every lesson and at all times. This happens even though girls and boys are usually taken together in most schools, therefore the important differences between the two must be taken into account.

THE GIRL AND STANCE

PART I. THE BEGINNING

Before the girl begins to develop she must acquire the erect flexible back necessary for classical dance, so that later she will be able to maintain the fully lifted torso and straightened but still flexible spine. This is particularly important in England where children usually lose their "baby tummy" later than elsewhere. To achieve the "feeling" of correct stance the following exercise has been evolved and is introduced before the first *plié* of a class.

9

Figure 3. Open arms to second and turn legs outward. The girl on the left is a little too far back on her heels.

slightly forward stance is resumed as the child stretches upwards from the *plié* (figure 3).

N.B. Degrees of turn-out required during the first stages of training follow later (see p. 26).

PART 2. STANCE WHEN THE GIRL BEGINS TO DEVELOP

Immediately the girl begins to develop her bust and/or buttocks four slight changes must be made in the elementary stance:—

Begin as in 1 and 2 above p. 9, but as the girl rises to *demi-pointe* she must raise the growing bust by using the muscles within the lower ribs and carefully maintain correct breathing by using both intercostal and accessory respiratory muscles so that the chest expands outwards and sideways – NOT upwards and downwards. By so using these sets of muscles the upper rib cage is better able to carry the growing breast. On no account must the chest itself be raised by an upwards thrust of the breast-bone and a pinching backwards of the shoulders.

It is also at this stage in training that the shoulder-blades must be encouraged to slide downwards along the spine and the upper chest be opened outwards by a correct intake and exhalation of breath. Once the correct stance can be sustained by firm control of all the muscles in trunk and thighs, the chest is held quietly still in position and the arm movement commences in the shoulder socket and NOT in the shoulder itself, which should remain still.

The head now needs another slight lift upwards so that the centre line of balance will run through from the crown of the head and be poised over the insteps as it was in the first stage of finding the correct stance. i.e. before the rise to *demi-pointe*. This means that the shoulders should now be directly over the hips and not just in front of them as they were before the bust began to grow (figure 4).

1. Stand erect, feet close but not pressed together and pointing straight forward (i.e. not turned-out). Knees must be directly above the toes, weight balanced over the three points of the foot (i.e. big and little toe joints and heel). Arms hang softly to sides, spine is pulled up to its straightest and crown of the

Figure 1. Stand erect, feet straight.

Figure 2. Rise to *demi-pointe*, arms to first position.

head should be directly over the insteps. Eyes directed forward and focussing something opposite their own level (figure 1).

N.B. At this stage there should be no lift of the chest. The spine alone is stretched upwards with the head poised freely.

2. Breathe in and rise to *demi-pointe* (no higher) thus carrying the weight more forward over the balls of the feet and simultaneously raise arms to first position, no higher than breast-bone (figure 2). (The difference between boys' and girls' hands is noted later.)

3. Lower heels, but maintain weight more forward over balls of feet so that centre line of balance now runs from the crown of the head to rest over the balls of the feet. The stomach muscles and those inside the thigh must be pulled upwards, and those of the buttocks pulled downwards and inwards if this position and balance are to be maintained.

N.B. Ideally once the boy or girl is correctly poised on *demi-pointe* all that is done is to lower the heels without moving any other part of the body.

4. Open arms to second position and turn legs outwards from the hip-joint into first position still trying to keep weight forward and stance as before. At this point it may be necessary for some girls to lift their heads a little higher and refocus the eyes. This is usually the case for those with short necks. From this first position *pliés* should commence. Care must be taken that the same erect,

Figure 4. As soon as the girl can "feel" this new adult stance.

As soon as the girl can "feel" this new "adult" stance, she must hold the chest firmly and freely opened outwards by breathing deeply, so that the diaphragm as well as the intercostal and accessory respiratory muscles support the rib-cage, which carries the breast.

In addition, at this stage in acquiring "adult" stance, the girl must stretch her entire spine fully upwards from the waist and stretch her legs fully outwards and away from the hip-socket, so that the muscles around and within the pelvis and stomach are kept fully active (i.e. in a state of tonicity). The body will then be free to move in any direction from the waist upwards and the legs to move more freely and away from the so-called "gap" between hip-socket and waist (see p. 61). The pelvis must only be allowed to tilt forwards from the hip-joints and never "rock" backwards whenever a curve in the spine is required for such poses as an *arabesque*. The proper line for this will be attained by correctly using the hinge at the hip-joint (i.e. the forwards tilt of the pelvis and the curve upwards and backwards of the spine from above the waist (figure 15). The same pull out of the waist and the leg away from the hip-socket is also essential for any *développé* or lift of the working leg to the side and, particularly, in front. Without it the pelvis will twist or "rock" and the spine lose its erect stance.

THE BOY AND STANCE AND POSITION OF BOY'S AND GIRL'S ARMS AND HANDS

The boy should also use the first part of the exercise on girl's stance to obtain his correct stance so that his weight is properly placed, but when his spine is fully stretched and he matures the difference between his stance and that of the girl must be clearly defined, because he does not have to carry the extra weight of breast and buttocks at any time during his development.

When a boy's body begins to mature it is therefore more easily held erect than a girl's because of its normal physical shape. But because boys often lose their "baby tummy" later than girls, it is essential that they cultivate the masculine stance for classical dance during the first lessons. They must be trained to "feel" that when the spine is straightened to its fullest extent and thus erect, the shoulders are held over, but JUST IN FRONT OF the hips, chest expanded and shoulders pulled outwards from the chest which is expanded, and shoulder-blades pressed

Figure 5. Boys' spines at fullest stretch with shoulders over, but just in front of hips.

downwards along the spine. This brings the weight forward over the three points of balance of the foot (i.e. over the metatarsal arch and heel. See figure 5).

Because the boy does not, and has no need to possess so flexible a back as a girl, it is essential that he is made aware very early of the slight adjustments in balance needed when raising the working leg to back or side. His centre of balance when on two feet and standing correctly (with feet not turned-out) should be seen to run directly from the BACK of the crown of his head through his spine to that point where he balances himself over the centre of his feet; i.e. slightly more forward than the girl (figure 6).

Her centre should run from the centre of the crown of her head through the spine to where she also balances herself over the centre of her feet. The slight difference between the boy's and girl's stance is more obvious when the feet are fully turned-out. The boy appears to be very slightly in front of the perpendicular. The girl would be equally so if she did not lift her lower ribs upwards further than the boy in her efforts to straighten the lower part of her spine, (i.e. flatten the pelvis by pulling more strongly on her buttock muscles). By so doing and because she must stabilise her breast, the girl stretches her rib-cage upwards so that the crown of her head moves very slightly backwards and thus comes over the true perpendicular line.

13

Figure 6. First and last boys are just in front of the perpendicular.

N.B. The above more forwards stance is particularly important for both boys and girls with tight ham-strings (usually accompanying sway-back legs) as it prevents them pulling the knees too far backwards when they tighten the muscles. The forwards stance gives a little more flexibility and can increase the size of the *demi-plié* because the muscles at both the front and back of the legs and body equally maintain the stance.

1. THE POSITION OF THE BOY'S ARMS AND HANDS

1. The boy compensates for the slightly forwards stance of his body by the way in which he holds his arms and hands. His shoulders, usually being broader than a girl's, must be seen to be broad as this gives strength to the torso. To achieve this the curve of the arm in first position follows the natural line of the shoulder slightly downwards, so that the finger-tips are level with the diaphragm, but are the breadth of the forehead apart (figure 7). If he then raises his arms to fifth position, he should find that his finger-tips are over and just in front of the crown of his head and still the width of his forehead apart (i.e. they are roughly above his ears and by lifting his eyes he can just see inside his hands), (figures 8 and 9). This particular position ensures that his shoulders remain still as his arms move, i.e. his shoulders are pulled away from the socket, the shoulder-blades are pressed down the spine and strongly held.

2. A male hand must be cultivated from the beginning. It must be flatter than a girl's with palms facing directly forwards when in second position, or downwards according to the line required. If the hand is proffered to give a handshake, it falls naturally into the correct position (figures 10 and 11).

14

Figure 7. Boys' arms in first position. Finger-tips level with breast bone.

Figure 8. Boys' arms in fifth position. Centre boy has still to control his thumbs.

Figure 9. Girls' arms in fifth position.

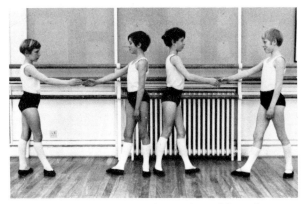

Figure 10. A male hand must be cultivated.

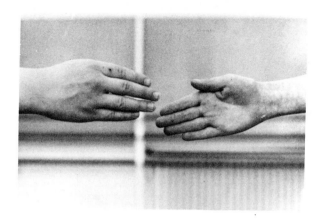

Fig. 11. "A little too stiff".

2. POSITION OF THE GIRL'S ARMS AND HANDS

The girl's arms and hands have to be altogether more rounded and move more smoothly than a boy's. They should never appear tense and only straighten appropriately for an *arabesque*, as do the boy's. They should always be held so that the elbows are just in front of the shoulders. In general the shape of each individual's shoulders helps to indicate the line the arm should take. But if the shoulders are very square, there should be a slight lowering of the arm.

To find the correct positions, the girl must stand correctly, the arms hanging relaxed at the sides. Allow the fingers to group softly; slightly round the elbows, bringing the arms forwards and round the body until the middle finger-tips are about four inches apart and about six inches from the body (the eyes should be able to see inside the palms without the head being lowered). The hands are now *bras bas*. Raise both arms without moving the shoulders and still rounded until the finger-tips are opposite the diaphragm. They should slope slightly downwards, thus following the line of the shoulder downwards. The arms are now in first position. Still maintaining the rounded arms, raise them without moving the shoulders until they are curved above, but in front of the head when, if the eyes are raised, they look into the palms (i.e. about nine inches above the head but about six inches from the perpendicular). The arms are now in fifth position. Return arms to first as above and open directly still rounded to second when, if the head is turned sideways, the eyes should be able to glance down the back of the arm from shoulder to elbow (figures 5, 6, 7, 8 and 9).

From the above four positions all other poses and *ports de bras* can be performed, except those used in preparation for *pirouettes*.

The Use of the Shortened First Position

Both boy and girl should understand how to control the arms in a shortened first position when using them as a preparation for and during *pirouettes* because if the arms are held in a correct first position they tend to pull the body forwards, and cannot be so held later when performing double-work. To help the children "feel" the shortened position it is useful to make them stand correctly with back to a wall or lying flat on the floor. Place arms in correct second. Draw finger-tips towards each other by moving the forearm only from the elbow. When the angle thus formed makes it difficult to maintain the rounded look of the arms, bring the whole arm more slightly forwards from the shoulders until the finger-tips are correctly placed (i.e. the girl's all-but touching and the boy's the width of his forehead apart).

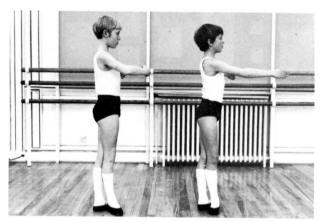

Figure 12. Use of shortened first position for *pirouettes.* First boy using normal position, second boy using first as a preparation.

A *pirouette* should begin with the preparatory arm being drawn into the shortened first the other arm still held in second then, without any movement from the shoulders, the preparatory arm moves to second as the dancer rises (boys) and *relevé* (girls) to *demi-* or full *pointe* simultaneously as the dancer begins to turn. This controlled opening and closing into a shortened first ensures the stability of the turn and prevents the dancer's stance and balance being upset by the "force" of the shoulder coming into the turn (figure 12; see also pp. 41 and 129).

4. ANOTHER VITAL ASPECT OF STANCE

Another vital aspect to the acquisition of correct stance for those hoping to become professionals is not always fully understood. The fully stretched spine and erect but flexible carriage of the body and head alert the audience to the presence of a dancer in command of self and technique. An attitude of mind and body most aptly summed up by Tamara Karsavina, that great artist: "Her shoes belong to her, the stage is hers".

It is difficult to make children understand this aspect of performance because few can imagine what it is like to experience that first moment of coming on stage to meet an audience waiting expectantly for their arrival. It does not matter whether it is as a classical dancer coming on to perform his or her one and only solo, as a member of the *corps de ballet*, or as some character. The very carriage of that dancer's head, eyes and body, alert and alive to the situation, should make the audience aware that he or she has something to give. It is for this reason that teachers must emphasise the utmost importance of all head movements. Exercises must be given encouraging its use to indicate and/or anticipate the line each movement will take.

Because the head is the heaviest part of the body children must be taught to balance it properly at all times. Without training they do this instinctively. But once the spine is more fully stretched upwards and the legs turned outwards, they usually begin to tense head, neck, shoulders and arms. This is most obvious when they appear on stage for the first time. Instead of the four walls of the familiar hall or studio, they face a black empty "hole". If the stage is "raked" the tension is worse. Yet it should not cause tension if the children have been taught to use the head freely and appropriately either to centre or counter-balance limbs and body. Even some professionals are not guided properly to practise the subtle adjustments needed when working on a "rake". Yet the very slight lift or backwards tilt of the head when entering and perhaps coming down stage not only helps the dancer to sustain a pose, but also allows the audience from gallery to stalls to see that he or she is able to cope with the dance in hand.

2

PHYSICAL FACTORS

I. THE TILT OF THE PELVIS

To ensure a correct "tilt" of the pelvis forwards, both boy and girl must be trained very early to use the natural hinge-like movement between body and leg at the hip-joint. To achieve this the child stands erect in first position, not turned-out, breathes in correctly to slim the waist by stretching upwards without raising the shoulders, then bends forwards as far as possible with an absolutely straight back and without moving the head, which is in line with the spine.

Figure 13. The girl tilts to a right angle. (She has pitched back a little because the thigh muscles are insufficiently pulled up, but the angle is correct.)

Figure 14. The boy. Note how a perfect angle is made if the body and legs are fully stretched.

The pelvis alone "tilts" forwards so that the body forms an angle with the legs at the hip-joint and does not have any curve (figures 13–14). Once children understand and can hold their bodies at this angle with their legs, they will be better able to achieve and hold an *arabesque*. In this the supporting leg must be absolutely perpendicular to the floor, whilst the pelvis lies roughly at right angles to the supporting leg and is parallel to the floor; the body is curved upwards and slightly backwards from above the waist.

19

Thus, in *arabesque* the raised leg is counter-balanced by the body and head, because both are equally distributed over the supporting leg (figure 15, see also p. 36).

Figure 15. There is a proper tilt of the pelvis forward in an *arabesque*.

2. THE CORRECT RISE TO DEMI-POINTE

Although all children must understand the need to stand on the three points of balance when the whole foot is on the floor (i.e. across the metatarsal arch and heel) the moment they rise to *demi-pointe*, they must be able to "feel" that the weight is now carried over the centre of the foot, i.e. straight through the shin-bone and over the three bigger toes (children with an extra long big toe require great care over this movement). In some cases, the little toe will not even rest on the floor, as the foot naturally slopes away and if the child attempts to keep the little toe on the floor, the foot rolls outwards and weakens ankle and

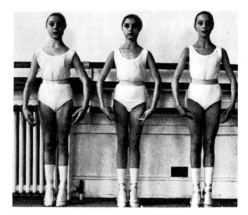

Figure 16. Correct rise to *demi-pointe*. Left, a straight line runs from hip to knee and centre of foot.

Figure 17. Correct rise to *demi-pointe* retaining centre line and slightly forward movement. (The child on the left is pressing on her little toes.)

20

arch. The central balance on *demi-pointe* is most important for all types of foot, particularly those with very high arches (figures 16, 17 and p. 39).

3. PRESSURE INTO AND OUT OF THE FLOOR

A correct rise on to *demi-pointe* for balance, *pirouettes* or any form of jump will only be obtained if the child realises the need to push into and immediately straight out of the floor with the preparatory *plié*. The pressure must be exerted straight from the knee downwards through the shin-bone to the whole foot from heel to arch and toes; then immediately the heel is about to leave the floor as if going into a full *plié* the reverse action must begin. i.e. the heel presses into the floor, the muscles under the foot react and contract to push the foot out of the floor up to three-quarter *pointes* and push the whole leg and then body into

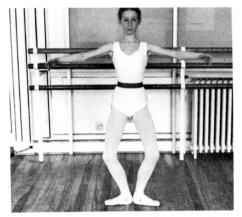

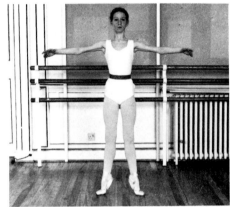

(*a*) *demi-plié*.   (*b*) rise through *demi-pointes*.

Figure 18. Pressure into and out of the floor during preparation for a jump in first position.

Figure 19. The jump in first position.

the air. The knee simultaneously straightens, causing all the muscles above to react and push the body and head upwards (figures 18a, 18b, 19 and p. 80). It should

21

be understood that whereas great pressure from the knee downwards must be put into the floor before the foot can react, there must also be a strong push upwards from the heel and thus from the knee as soon as the rise or jump begins (see p. 80 for *demi-plié*).

4. THE SUPPORTING LEG AND TRANSFER OF WEIGHT

The placing of weight directly over the supporting leg is an item frequently neglected during the first stages of training. This is particularly noticeable in *battements tendus* when the child tends to carry some weight over to the working toe instead of balancing it correctly over the supporting leg and maintaining the fully stretched spine.

The child must be taught to recognise the subtle differences in the transfer of weight which takes place when the foot moves from first position to the side and when it moves from fifth position to the side.

(a) *From first*. When the dancer stands in first position the central line of balance runs from the crown of the head to a point between the two heels. Therefore, as the foot moves sideways a very slight transfer of weight on to the supporting leg must be seen to take place. The central line of balance now runs from the crown of the head to the instep of the supporting leg, i.e. if the body is

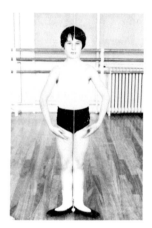

Figure 20. Feet in first position. Centre line from crown of head runs down between two feet.

Figure 21. Transfer over to supporting leg when performing *pointe tendue*. Note: leg has moved slightly away from plumb line demonstrating transfer of weight.

held correctly and pulled fully upwards from the waist and the working leg fully stretched outwards from the hip (figures 20, 21).

(b) *From fifth*. When the dancer stands in fifth position, the central line of balance runs from the crown of the head to a point between the two insteps;

22

therefore, when the foot moves sideways there should be no apparent transfer of weight on to the supporting leg because the central line of balance should

Figure 22. Feet in fifth position. Arms slightly wide to show line of leg and are strained.

Figure 23. Pointe tendue. Centre line of balance remains in same place.

remain in the same place, i.e. if the body is held correctly and fully pulled up and both legs *equally* turned-out (figures 22, 23).

In both (a) and (b) the working foot returns to the correct position without an extra movement of either leg and without any sinking of the body into the hips. Thus in (a) there will be a slight transfer of weight so that the central line again falls between the two heels; and in (b) there will be no movement at all (see also p. 39).

The transfer and maintenance of weight correctly over the supporting leg places some strain on all a child's muscles in the region between hip-joint and waist and whenever the working foot loses contact with the floor. It is for this reason that all early training must stress the need for a complete pull upwards from the waist and an outwards, downwards pull from the hip-joint. This is of vital importance to both boy and girl and best results are obtained if more exercises are given to the side only and from first position, for when lifting the working leg to the side at any angle up to 90°, it is easy to correct the straightening of the spine, the angle of pelvis and hip, and the pulling away of the working leg without any displacement of weight.

Another important exercise to use for an understanding of the correct transfer of weight is raising the working leg from first position or fifth position to *retiré* at 90°. As in *battements tendus* when moving from first position, the slight transfer of weight can be seen to occur as the working foot is raised directly upwards along the side of the supporting leg and the central line of balance passes from the crown of the head over to the instep of the supporting foot. But when the working toe is raised from fifth position up the front or back to the side of the supporting leg, there should be no movement whatsoever in any part of the body save the working leg, where there is an outwards pull on the inside and an inward pull on the outside muscles.

5. THE STRAIGHT LINE OF THE RAISED LEG

When the child first begins exercises in which the working leg is raised at any degree from the floor, the straight line running through the leg by way of

Figure 24. The straight line of raised leg. The leg is about to be lifted.

the bones from hip-joint to the centre of the foot must be maintained (figure 24). To achieve this the child must "feel" that the leg is being pulled outwards and is turned-out from the hip-socket, the hips remaining square and the body stretched upwards from the waist if the leg is raised front. If the leg is raised to the side at any angle up to 90° the same conditions apply. If however, and at a later stage, the leg is raised any higher than 90° the pelvis does tilt very slightly upwards on the side of the raised leg. At 90° the pelvis should remain flat and level provided the child does not "sickle" the foot in any way. The tendency to "push the heel forwards" by an independent movement at the ankle usually "rocks" the pelvis (i.e. pushes it forwards with the resultant arched back) because the "Tail is tucked in" in an effort to bring the heel forwards and this way of achieving a turn-out inhibits the muscles working in the buttocks and abdomen, which need to be in a state of tonicity if they are to play their proper part in any movement.

If the straight line of the leg from hip to toe is maintained with a correct turn-out, then the knees and the front of the whole foot should face the ceiling when the working leg is raised or placed at any angle to the side. The outwards "sickled" foot distorts the line in any kind of *ronde de jambe*, as it tends to make

24

the dancer turn away from the supporting leg, thus throwing the whole supporting side out of alignment. Similarly the inwards "sickled" foot distorts the line because it brings extra pressure on to the outside of the leg and this inhibits the inner muscles of both working and supporting legs.

6. OTHER ASPECTS OF TILTING THE PELVIS

When teaching how to tilt the pelvis, teachers must ensure that it only moves directly forwards and downwards or upwards at the hip-joints, i.e. when pulling the "tail" down and spinal column and head upwards, the pelvis is slightly tilted upwards at the front (figures 1 and 2). When bending the body forwards to a clear right-angle it should be held in the same position because the thigh and pelvis act like a hinge (figures 13 and 14). If it is "rocked" by arching the spine at waist level, the legs will move backwards and the body be out of balance. So if the subtle movement is to be correct, the entire spine must be kept fully stretched so that the child can feel how to counterbalance the weight of the body coming forwards by trying to control all the muscles of the inner and outer thighs as well as those of the legs and feet. It also helps them to understand why the pelvis must in no way twist. This is particularly important when working on turn-out, where any twisting throws the entire body out of alignment at some point. Thus in the early stages of training the teacher should ensure that each child uses whatever turn-out is possible and that it takes places from the hip-joints only.

It is not easy for any child to control the pelvis so that it never moves except at some angle forwards from the erect position until it is at a right-angle to the legs. The body can descend further. But that can only happen as it curves slightly inwards, led by the head and towards the ankles. This happens because (see p. 18) the head is the heaviest part of the body and instinctively finds the centre of balance if correctly poised (figures 15–17). It is for this reason that the flexibility of the upper spine and head cannot be stressed too frequently. But if it is to be so, then control over the pelvis is all important. It is the only part of the body which should remain parallel to the floor, the only other stable part of a dancer's equipment. Children find this idea difficult because few today are taught about the forces of gravity. But it does help to explain how and why the head, pelvis and one or two feet are essentially always part of the central line of balance, whether firmly placed on the floor, soaring in the air, or landing from one of the five jumps.

3

DEGREES OF TURN-OUT

BEFORE both boy and girl are able to sustain their correct stance throughout any exercise, the degree of turn-out should be limited by the child's own physical capacity for turning the entire leg outwards from the hip-joint whilst maintaining the erect back without any "rolling" of the feet or pushing forwards of the pelvis by the so-called "tucking-in" of the tail. This last movement can be dangerous as it leads to a tensing and stiffening of the buttock and stomach muscles. However once boy and girl are able to sustain the correct stance, then the degree of turn-out should be increased to 90° (i.e. with each foot).

A careful assessment of each child's physique should be made before the preliminary degree of turn-out is decided and in no case should this be less than each foot at 45°, although the angle of 60° is best if it can be sustained. The following may be of help.

I. THE SWAY-BACK LEG

The child with sway-back legs should not be encouraged to turn-out fully until the stance is firmly established at 75° (i.e. each foot). This does not usually occur until the girl is well-developed but may still be growing. Such children, if turned-out too soon can develop "rolling" feet, weak ankles and the dangerous "rock" of the pelvis as well as the forwards thrust of the chest. To counteract this they must be taught to stand firmly on the three points of balance of the feet at 45° (at the beginning of training) with the knees directly over the toes and under the hips. The knees must not be allowed to pull back too far when tightening. This can only be prevented by keeping the weight on the BALLS of the foot with spine straight and by a strong pull upwards of the muscles inside the upper leg (i.e. adductor, longus satorius and gracilis).

Such children should be restricted to lifting the working leg no higher than 90° so that the supporting leg remains perpendicular to the floor. This ensures that when the working leg is raised or extended into an *arabesque*, there is a proper tilt of the pelvis forwards (and not a "rock"), as well as a strong pull outwards of the working leg away from the hip-joint in order to maintain balance (figure 15).

When rising to *demi-pointe* children with sway-back legs must hold their weight upwards and centred over the balls of the feet and rise NO HIGHER THAN *demi-pointe* until such time when the stance is fully established because they show a tendency to roll outwards at the ankle and thus place too much weight on the little toe and not over the three bigger toes (see p. 20).

26

Another valuable corrective for sway-back legs is NOT to allow such children to stand with their heels pressed together in first position as this prevents the inner thigh muscles from working strongly and tends to throw the pelvis forwards. Instead they should stand with heels a little way apart. The distance is determined by the degree of sway-back and the thickness of the upper parts of the legs, which should touch, but not be pressed together. The slight gap between the heels helps to pull the thigh and inner muscles of the legs upwards and outwards. It also helps to prevent a too strong pull back of the knees, which can then be pulled more upwards and – if the weight is correctly placed – slightly forwards. But this gap must be closed as soon as stance is firmly established.

2. KNOCK KNEES

Children with knock-knees should not be encouraged to turn-out fully until the correct stance is established with the feet at 75° (i.e. each foot). As well as being taught to stand firmly on the three points of balance with the feet at 60° (this angle is more valuable than 45° at the preliminary stage), they must be encouraged to pull the knees outwards and round over the toes by drawing the buttock muscles upwards and together, and pulling the muscles INSIDE the upper leg forwards and outwards.

This can only be achieved by bringing the weight more forwards over the balls of the feet (when flat) and maintaining this more forwards stance and strongly pulled up spine when rising on to *demi-pointe*, NO HIGHER (see p. 20).

Figure 25. The body must be centred between the two feet and knees correctly placed over the toes.

Figure 26. Fourth opposite fifth.

For such children it is valuable to use exercises where the legs often drop in *demi-pliés* in the open position (figure 25). Whenever this drop occurs, the body must be seen to be centred between the two feet and the knees correctly placed over the toes without any displacement of the spine, and above all with the working foot placed squarely on the three points of balance of the foot when flat, as such children have a greater tendency to "roll" inwards than any others.

N.B. Fourth opposite fifth position produces better results than fourth opposite first (figure 26) to obtain this central balance when in *demi-plié*. But it should be noted that fourth opposite fifth position either for *demi-* or full *plié* is a particularly difficult position and should not be practised until stance is firmly established, turn-out is stable, there is a good understanding of the relationship between the various parts of the leg – in particular to keep the hips square whilst ensuring that both knees are well pressed outwards towards and almost over their respective toes – and the body is firmly and equally held over both feet (figure 27).

Figure 27. Keeping hips square while ensuring both knees are almost over their respective toes.

Figure 28. Fourth opposite first.

Fourth opposite first position can be used more safely; but not until the child does understand stance and how to maintain turn-out. This is particularly so with knock-kneed children, who tend to be close-hipped and these, above all, must understand how to maintain a reasonable turn-out even before attempting fourth opposite first (figure 28).

Exercises using *retirés devant, derrière* and *passé* are also valuable if care is taken to ensure that the working knee is raised directly to hip level with the same degree of turn-out as it leaves the floor, is held momentarily and returns to first or fifth position. (There must be no movement of the supporting leg or body, except the slight transfer on to the supporting leg from first position.) This can only happen if all the muscles of the supporting side of the leg and body are firmly pulled upwards with the knee directly over and facing the same plane as the toe, a particularly difficult position for those with sway-back legs, which need more than average care (figures 29, 30).

Children with knock-knees seem to benefit more from lying flat on the floor with legs perfectly straight and turned outwards from the hips than from lying in "Frogs". When lying straight they should be encouraged to rotate the entire leg outwards and inwards up to twenty times with the legs fully stretched (figures 31, 32).

N.B. Toes frequently leave the floor and should be allowed to do this freely when lying and turned-in.

Figure 29. Raising leg to hip level in *retiré* is very difficult at this age, as muscles are not yet strong enough to hold hips level.

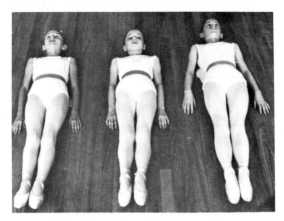

Figure 31. Rotate whole leg inwards.

Figure 30. The same degree of turn-out as the foot leaves the floor.

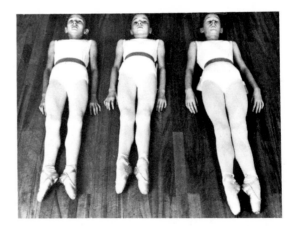

Figure 32. Rotate whole leg outwards.

Figure 33. Examples of the three different types of foot
referred to.

All such children must be taught to keep their weight correctly over the
three points of their feet and NOT BE PERMITTED TO RISE HIGHER THAN *demi-
pointe* until such time as the correct stance becomes habitual and they are seen
to carry their weight correctly forwards at all times when rising to *demi-pointe*.
With all such children attention must be focussed on the correct use of all the
toes and the need to balance over the centre of the foot. In addition, those with
the over-arched foot must strengthen their ankles and toes, and be encouraged
NEVER to rise too high except on to *pointes*, when the arch must be firmly controlled (figures 34a), b), c), d), e).)

Insufficient use is made of the correct *demi-pointe* position. When teaching
children to rise through the centre of the whole foot, they must be made to
understand there are three distinct points of balance before the full *pointe* position
is reached namely:—

Quarter pointe. The heel is just raised from the floor and the weight of the
body rests across the toes to the back of the ball of the foot (figure 34b).)

Half (Demi-) pointe. The weight rests directly across the metatarsal arch and
this is the most important point of balance for all beginners. Moreover any
children with over-arched feet, weak metatarsal arches, long slim toes or fore-
foot, or the too long big toe should never rise beyond this point until instep,
ankle and toes have been strengthened and they are ready to *relevé sur les pointes*
(figure 34c).)

Three-quarter pointe. The weight rests virtually below the metatarsal arch and
the tips of the toes: i.e. more or less on the toes alone and can therefore be a
highly dangerous point of balance except for those with exceptionally strong
feet (figure 34d).)

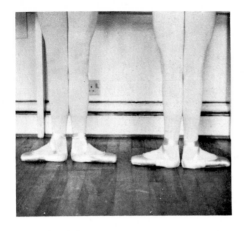

(a) Flat feet

(b) ¼ *pointes*

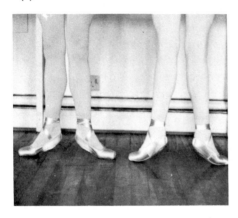

(c) ½ *pointes*

(d) ¾ *pointes*

(e) full *pointes*

Figure 34.

Full Pointe. The foot now rests on the tips of the toes. i.e. that tiny padded section at the top of the bones and protected by the nail. All the muscles of the leg from that point to the thighs must be pulled upwards, together with all the muscles from the waist, if the weight is to be held away from this delicate point of balance (figure 34e).)

4. THE CHILD WITH THE UNEQUAL LENGTH OF LEG

There seems to be a growing percentage of children with one leg longer than the other and these children must concentrate much harder on the correct transfer of weight and stance. The first thing to master is to hold themselves well-lifted on the longer leg and attempt to pull the short leg outwards and downwards from the hip, instead of their usual practice of shortening the longer leg by sinking into the hip-joint and failing to maintain the "gap" between waist and hip. Such children are comparatively easy to recognise. Teachers should look at each child standing erect in front of them. Their legs must not be turned-out. Look for an uneven shoulder line, or for an uneven level at the pelvic waistline.

An attempt must be made to correct this inequality at the very beginning of training. This shortening may be due to the current practice of always carrying a brief-case (often heavy with school books) with one hand, or a shoulder-bag always on one shoulder. If this is the cause of shortening then much greater attention must be paid to the shoulder-line and set of the hips by increasing the length between arm-pit on the short side, and to a strengthening of the muscles round the waist in order to maintain the balance of the pelvis over the hip-joints. Such children should never be allowed to "rock" the pelvis, nor the upper part of the spine in an *arabesque* nor raise the leg above 90° until such time as their muscles can be held in a long adagio.

4

GROWTH AND CONTROL OVER LIMBS

As yet is is impossible to predict how a child will grow. It is therefore important to take into account the usual pattern of development in an average child and particularly the difference between boy and girl when studying classical dance.

1. THE GIRL. Because the girl has to be taught to carry the extra weight of bust and buttocks, and has to have a more flexible body movement than the boy, it is essential that she is encouraged to strengthen and stretch all her muscles as much as she can before she begins to develop by controlling the height at which she holds the working leg and to extend this leg as far as possible away from her body without sinking into the supporting hip. She should therefore

Figure 35. This girl should be able to hold her leg in *adagio* at 90°.

Figure 36. The boy should be able to hold his leg in *adagio* at 45°. There is still insufficient strength to hold the hips firm at his age.

be able to hold her leg in adagio at 90° and throw it above that angle before she starts to develop (figure 35).

2. THE BOY. The boy on the other hand does not have to learn to carry extra weight, but he does ultimately have to lift the girl, therefore he must be taught to strengthen all his muscles, particularly those of the back, and to broaden his shoulders before he begins to develop. Moreover the boy studying classical dance usually seems to lengthen in the leg before the rest of his body grows,

which frequently makes him appear to lose control over stance, legs and arms.

It is therefore advisable that the boy should be able to hold the leg no higher than 45° in adagio and throw it no higher than 90° whenever his legs appear too long in proportion to the rest of his body (figure 36).

1. THE POSITION OF THE HAND ON THE BARRE

The position of the hand on the barre is all important if stance is to be correct with shoulders level and chest expanded sideways. The exact placing will vary according to the length of the child's arm as it grows, therefore it must be periodically adjusted because unequal growth presents difficulties.

To find the ideal position it is usually best to stand the child about eighteen inches from the barre in the correct stance, but with the feet pointing forwards (see p. 9). Raise arms to first position, then open both arms until they are midway between first and second (i.e. at 45° to the body). Bend elbow on supporting side, lowering it slightly but keeping it well away from body. Now place the hand lightly on the barre, so that the thumbs rest along the fingers ON TOP OF, BUT NOT GRASPING the barre as this causes tension across the shoulders. This placing may well mean that the child has to move slightly nearer or further

Figure 37. The exact distance depends very much on length of upper arm. The boy at the back is 2½ inches taller than the one in front.

from the barre. The exact distance depends very much on the length of the upper arm, which, in a number of cases lengthens at a later stage than the forearm (figure 37).

The correct position at the barre should be such that the hand need not be moved to and fro, except with the slight movement forwards when the leg is raised at the back which is particularly important for those whose upper arm is short. But in no circumstances must the supporting elbow be allowed to twist upwards as this distorts the shoulder line, which in its turn twists the spine.

2. THE CARRIAGE OF THE HEAD AND THE FOCUS OF THE EYES

Because a child grows unpredictably, it cannot always feel and adjust itself to what is sometimes a quick lengthening of limb and/or body, therefore constant care must be taken to ensure that it holds its head correctly and focusses its eyes at the right level. It has been found that because children, particularly boys, grow by fits and starts, they usually leave the eyes focussed on some familiar spot instead of re-focussing a little higher to compensate for the newly acquired height. Thus they do not stretch the spine upwards to the fullest extent. The head then appears to droop and the eyes are cast down. The head must at all

Figure 38. The focus of the eyes. From left to right, too low, correct, too high.

times be encouraged to move freely. It helps to teach children to watch the lines made by hands and arms (figure 38).

Children must be taught to make every effort to adjust themselves to their new height, particularly in professional schools, where the daily lesson in familiar surroundings tends to make them careless. They must be constantly alert to the need for full co-ordination of body movement within the space allowed.

3. THE STRENGTHENING OF THE SPINE

The strengthening and control of the spine together with the turn-out are the most important items to study in the early stages. The child must be made to understand that the spine from just below the shoulder-blades to the coccyx (i.e. "tail") must be held as straight and as still as possible and that any curve or bend forwards or backwards should be made from just above the waist and NOT at the waist-line, (i.e. just below the shoulder-blades). This curve or bend can be cultivated by concentrating on the correct intake and exhalation of breath, which helps the child to understand the important part to be played by the intercostal and accessory respiratory muscles (see p. 62).

The first point to make when straightening the lower half of the spine (i.e. from just above the waist to the "tail") is to insist the child does not "sink"

35

into a *demi-* or full *plié*, but "pulls the tail" directly downwards as the knees relax outwards over the toes and under the hip-joints (figure 25), and on returning

Figure 39. The hips remain facing the same plane, but not quite at the same level, when raising the leg in second position. This is very difficult at the age of 12.

to the erect position the weight of the body must be pushed straight upwards by pressing the heels into the floor and straightening the knees. In this way the child should be able to understand that the weight of the body, particularly when the girl begins to develop, must be carried upwards away from the legs by the strength of all the muscles from the top of the hips to the lower ribs, and by the careful stretch and strengthening of the spine.

The all too common fault of altering the lumbar curve by "tucking in the tail" to facilitate a greater turn-out whilst the *plié* descends results in the heels slipping forwards, thus causing over-turned feet which weakens the ankles. Moreover the coccyx curves under the torso, which not only inhibits the muscles of pelvis, stomach and waist, but also causes the child to "sit" in the *plié*. This is a bad fault which is impossible to correct in later stages of training, when there must be absolute control of the erect yet mobile spine required when preparing and landing from any kind of jump.

The tremendous importance of a strongly controlled spine is nowhere more in evidence than in an *arabesque*, where, with hips and shoulders facing the same plane, the working leg is seen to be equally balanced over the supporting leg. This happens only when the supporting leg is absolutely perpendicular with the pelvis more or less at right angles and lying roughly parallel to the floor, the spine stretched and lifted upwards. It is then that the true line of the *arabesque* can be held (figure 15).

5

FURTHER COMMENTS ON THE TEACHING OF BOYS

Because boys learn more slowly than girls, they must work more slowly in class and have less steps to study in a year, but they must be allowed to see the result of their work at the end of every class. For this reason during the last minutes of class they should be given their heads and be allowed to turn, leap or beat – or at least try something of that nature even though the movement has not been studied in class.

It is essential that boys should be kept moving and never allowed to stand about once the lesson has started. Once they have warmed their muscles, they must work to keep up that warmth. In this way their stamina and strength are built up more quickly. Moreover by constantly pushing the boy to work consistently and rhythmically during the lesson he is better able to contend with irregularities of growth and co-ordinate all his movements at all times.

1. MALE STANCE

Once the boy has firmly established his correct stance, he should be able to

Figure 40. He should be able to press his knees outwards in *demi-pliés* (first and second).

press the knees outwards and downwards into *demi-* and full *pliés* (figures 40, 41) or to rise more easily on to *demi-pointe*, or into a jump without that backwards throw of the body which frequently occurs when he has been allowed to press too firmly backwards on his heels before he has lost his "baby tummy" (i.e. he has probably "tucked in his tail"). This throwing backwards is particularly

Figure 41. And in full *pliés*.

noticeable during the first attempts at jumping in first and second position and in *changements*.

This does not mean that the boy need not worry about pushing into the floor with the heels. On the contrary – he must be made fully aware of the need to bring extra pressure to bear on the whole foot when moving into and out of the floor by using *demi-pliés* as the preparatory and finishing movement to every type of *pirouette* and jump. It is that extra firm push on to the heel and into the

Figure 42. The strong rise upwards in a *soubresaut*. Note the arms are strained, a common fault at this stage.

floor which gives the necessary impetus for the strong rise upwards required in these movements (figure 42).

Another important difference to be noted between a boy's and a girl's dance is that the former should always use a RISE on to the *demi-pointe* in order to raise his body into a *pirouette*, etc. If he uses a *relevé*, he will inevitably lose control over his back by jumping himself out of his erect position. He must feel the pressure from the floor throughout his body as he RISES. If he loses contact with the floor, his toes and metatarsal arch, usually being less sensitive than a girl's, fail to grip the surface and his back gives way at the waist. This happens because he must keep the BACK of the crown of his head over the metatarsal arch and NOT the centre of the crown as with the girls.

2. THE DIFFERENCE BETWEEN THE RISE AND THE RELEVÉ

Too little difference is made between the rise and the *relevé*. Although the terms are the same in the original French, in practice the movements are NOT identical. Children must be able to understand both movements. But the boy seldom, if ever, uses *relevé*. He must know exactly how to use a correct rise at all times.

Rise. The legs are straight and either turned-out or knees facing straight forwards (figure 2). The heels are then gradually pushed upwards from the floor, the toes remaining exactly in the same place as the foot stretches upwards through the quarter, half (*demi-*) until, if required, three-quarter point is reached. The weight is always centred through the bones of leg and feet. There is always a slight forwards movement of the whole body through the rise. Thus in first, third or fifth position, the heels are seen to be more or less apart at the height of the rise. When rising in second or fourth position they are slightly further apart. Under no circumstances must the toe move from the spot at which the rise begins.

Relevé. In *relevé* however, there must be a slight spring on to the three-quarter or full *pointe*. During this slight spring, the toes are brought directly under the central line of balance running from the head to the instep of one or both feet. The relationship of the legs does not change. Thus in *relevé* in first position, the heels should touch as they reach the highest point. In fifth position the legs are tightly drawn together. Whilst in second or fourth position the toes come slightly towards each other. i.e., during a *relevé* on two feet, the angle and relationship of the legs should not change because the little spring brings the tips of the toes roughly to that same spot over which the instep rested during the preparatory *demi-plié*.

3. TRANSFER OF WEIGHT

When transferring weight from two feet to one, the boy must still maintain the slightly forwards stance and lift the torso upwards from the waist in order to give the working leg greater freedom to move in the hip socket. This is why he should be taught to raise his leg very slowly from *pointe tendue* in any direction to an angle of 45° and then 90° before he uses *développés*.

It is only when a boy can control the height at which he holds his leg and acquires a certain degree of flexibility in the upper part of his spine that he should begin to use a true *arabesque* at 90° by "bowing" directly over the "hinge" (i.e. hip-joint) and by lifting the upper part of his body in order to keep his spine pulled upwards as far as possible, remembering also the essential small backwards curve of the upper part of the spine, which should NOT be so pronounced as with a girl.

4. BOY'S ARM IN ARABESQUE (figure 43)

Figure 43. Boy's arm during first stage of *arabesque*.

The sideways arm in *arabesque* should only be pressed further backwards into second and third position *arabesque* lines during the final years of training, as the backwards inclined line is generally considered too feminine. The backwards line is used only when the male dancer has learnt to keep his shoulders square as he turns the arm in its socket to take it backwards.

N.B. The movement for male dancers is usually made from first position, one arm stretching forwards and the other moving slightly downwards until it turns naturally in its socket to continue backwards.

5. THE MALE HAND AND ARM IN PIROUETTES

The use of the male arm in *pirouettes* is all important. The boy must understand the exact placing of his arms during the preparation and commencement of the turn. The front or preparatory arm is drawn into the shortened first position, i.e. if the arms are first opened correctly in second, the line across the back from elbow to elbow should hardly alter as the preparatory arm is drawn into first. This means that most movement takes place from the elbow inwards as the preparatory arm is drawn into first so that the fingertips will rest exactly opposite the diaphragm and are drawn towards its centre. From this position the preparatory arm is again swept out to second with the rise to *demi-pointe* at the same moment as the shoulder coming into the turn "gives force" and the opposite arm is also drawn towards the shortened first, so that both arms are firmly held rounded and together the moment the turn begins.

Pirouettes en dehors and en dedans for boys

Boys should first practise *pirouettes en dehors* from second finishing with the working foot closing in fifth *derrière*. But as soon as these are mastered it is

40

valuable to teach *pirouettes en dehors* from second but finishing firmly with the working foot in *retiré* before opening it to *pointe tendue* to the side, and then immediately dropping the foot into another *demi-plié* as a preparation for another *pirouette* finishing with the working foot closing in fifth as before.

Only after boys have mastered *pirouettes en dehors* should they practise *pirouettes en dedans* commencing from fourth opposite fifth and falling into a *demi-plié fourth en avant* to finish, arms opening to second after having been closed in the shortened first. The working leg should first be trained to circle from back to side before being brought into *retiré* just as the turn begins. At a later stage it is advisable for boys to practise moving the working leg from the preparatory position directly into *retiré*.

When boys begin to *pirouette* it is vital for them to understand the difference between the small and large open positions (see Ex. 6, p. 82). For *en dehors pirouettes* the small open positions are best. For *en dedans pirouettes* the large open positions and particularly the large fourth are most valuable for boys. It must be used so that in preparation the weight is firmly placed on the front leg *fondu*, the back leg being well braced so that it can spring up as the preparatory arm moves from first. Thus the working leg reaches second (before coming into *retiré* as both arms are likewise momentarily held in second, and then closed in shortened first. In this way both leg and arm coming into the *pirouette* help the dancer to take "force" without throwing the shoulders out of alignment (see Ex. 6, p. 82).

No boy should be allowed to turn with the working foot too low during the first years of training. The toes should be at least on a level with the bottom of the calf and firmly held at the centre of the working leg. It can be dangerous to hold the toes TOO FAR ACROSS the supporting leg as it tends to throw the boy off his centre line of balance as well as causing a turn-in of the raised leg.

Another vital point is that at this stage of training the boy should be turning on *demi-pointe* – NO HIGHER and NO LOWER (see p. 20).

6. STRETCHING BOYS

Never stretch a boy by violent exercise, particularly before he has lost his "baby tummy". It is considered best to use exercises with *Tirebouchon;* lunging forwards, sideways or backwards as far as possible, with both feet flat on the floor and recovering the upright position without bending the supporting leg; *grands battements* with a straight leg falling into an open position (see Ex. 17, p. 97); and quick *battements* (*glissés* and *grands*) moving into *demi-ronds de jambe en l'air* (figures 44, 45 and 46).

7. AS BOYS DEVELOP

The above points are of the utmost importance when the boy starts to develop. It is at this point in his growth when he frequently appears to lose co-ordination and control over his limbs. This can be due to his body growing faster than his

Figures 44–46. Lunging and other stretching exercises for boys.

Figure 44. Lunge forwards whilst stretching back leg.

Figure 45. Lunge whilst stretching sideways.

limbs or vice-versa; or (and this is fairly common) his legs growing faster than his arms. All this gives rise to loss of balance, turning-in, swaying back from the waist, etc. It is wise therefore to note that as soon as the boy starts to grow in one part more than another, or his voice starts to break, the following points must be insistently corrected.

(a) Knees must always be over toes and under the hips in all *pliés*, and the movements must be taken more slowly at the start of the lesson so that the heels are not allowed to rise from the floor until the last possible moment and return there as quickly as possible. That is on a count of eight; the heels should not rise until three; four is the lowest point and the heels return to the ground on

Figure 46. Lunge backwards whilst stretching front leg. Lunge is difficult at this stage, as boy rarely feels oblique line when moving backwards, only when moving forwards (*see figure 44*).

five; or as soon after as possible. It is also valuable to raise the arm in fifth at this stage, particularly during full *pliés* and *grands battements*.

(b) The foot must always make the fullest use of the floor so that the heel is always being pressed or pushed down and held.

(c) The leg should be controlled at various angles; i.e. 18° or 20° for all *battements glissés*, *frappés* and certain *fondu* exercises; at 45° for other *frappés*, *fondu* with *développé* and preparation for *flic-flac* exercises; at 90° NO HIGHER, for any full *développés*, *grands battements* and raising the leg from *pointe tendue* exercises. Even in those cases where the boy is naturally able to control a higher movement, the above rules are sacrosanct. A boy, who is naturally loose, all too easily loses control of his legs when he grows, and this can be more dangerous than with one who is stiff. Before a boy is allowed to use his legs freely, he must learn to control them. Height can only be gained when the boy can feel the natural lift of his back in *arabesque* and finally when he can adjust his own line of balance to his growth.

8. HEIGHT OF THE BOY'S ARM

The height of the boy's arm in second must be watched so that the shoulders are kept pulled outwards and pressed downwards with chest fully expanded and easy breathing. Careful attention should be paid to the freedom of the head, which tends at this period to become lazy or too free.

A useful way of helping boys to feel the need of stretching the arms, shoulders and chest outwards is to make them use a reverse *ports de bras* when practising *pliés*. First establish that they can use the normal *ports de bras* by insisting they take a correct second position before the *plié* begins. The arm must not go behind the shoulder line or be too high. It then lowers to *bras bas* absolutely centred at the depth of the *plié* and rises to first position as the legs are stretched before opening

43

again to second. Once this *port de bras* is mastered in all positions, the arm should be changed. It rises to fifth during the descent, lowers through first to *bras bas* during the stretch upwards and thence rises again to second. It is absolutely essential that the shoulders do not rise in any way and if the boy is viewed sideways, his profile should be clearly visible because the upper arm and elbow have been slightly opened away from the chest at the arm-pit, NOT the shoulder.

Raising the arm to fifth position in any type of *battement* to the front and particularly to the side is also very valuable as long as there is no raising of the shoulders. This helps boys to feel how freely the arms can work and how important it is to keep the upper arm opened away from the chest and not drawn in any way forwards, thus hiding the face (see figure 8 and compare the boy on left, who is not quite correct, with the one on right, who is).

9. ADAGIO FOR BOYS

Although boys in early lessons should not be given too many long adagios, that is exercises in which the pose has to be held for long periods or the leg is moved through many positions before descending to a closed position, they should be given a great deal of work where movements have to be sustained *en l'air* or, as in a very slow *pirouette*, *tours en l'air* and very slow jumps finishing in a well-held *demi-plié*.

Nevertheless within any *enchaînement* in adagio boys must be able to hold the position and/or pose not only at the end of the step, but on completion of every movement within it. For this reason a strong difference should be made between male and female phrasing of all adagios. It was explained by Fokine thus: "A girl performing a *développé* would be more likely to take four whole beats to complete the unfolding of the leg, whilst the boy would be expected to unfold for two beats and hold the pose for two beats. The girl might tend to hold her pose for another four beats, but the boy would continue towards another movement. She aims for the more lyrical unfolding of her line of dance, whilst he pauses more frequently to demonstrate the strength of his pose within that line".

10. TEACHING MALE JUMPS TO A MAZURKA

It is very useful to teach boys to jump firmly to a mazurka so that the strongest movement is upwards on the strongest beat (this is the correct accenting when dancing a traditional Polish Mazurka). 1. *Demi-plié*. 2. Jump and land in *demi-plié*. 3. Straighten knees (see Exercise 5, p. 82).

6

CONVENTIONS OF CLASSICAL DANCE

PERHAPS the most important things to be taken into account when training children in the co-ordination of movement is to develop their understanding of the classroom conventions which have gradually grown up through the work of leading teachers. Most of these derive from man's instinctive ways of balancing himself on one or two feet and may therefore be termed the natural laws of balance. There are two.

I. THE LAW OF OPPOSITION

The law of opposition was first noted by John Weaver (1723) as being an essential item in the training of dancers.

Always use the opposite arm to leg in front, no matter whether that leg is supporting or working with the hips facing the same plane as the shoulders

Figures 47–48. The law of opposition.

Figure 47. Pointe tendue croisé en avant.    *Figure 48. Arabesque croisé à terre.*

(i.e. as in walking, or in *arabesque* standing on the right leg, left raised behind or *à terre* and left arm in front (figures 47, 48).

The use of natural *épaulement* was first noted by Noverre (1760) as being essential to give line to certain movements and derived from man's natural proclivity to use his shoulders to swing forwards or backwards. (This was also noted by Weaver but not made essential.)

Always bring the same shoulder in front as leg in front, no matter whether that leg is working or supporting, when the dancer is travelling forwards or backwards, i.e. as in *petits jetés derrière* when the same shoulder comes forwards as the working foot lands on the floor to become the supporting leg. But in

Figure 49. The law of natural *épaulement*: same shoulder forward as foot in front.

petits jetés devant the same shoulder comes forwards as the working foot is raised sideways as the dancer travels backwards (figure 49).

3. CONVENTIONAL MOVEMENTS OF THE HEAD

The above laws of opposition and natural *épaulement* have given rise to the natural movements of the head which arise from the way people generally use it when travelling forwards or backwards.

(a) *The head when travelling forwards*

When travelling forwards the dancer usually TURNS the head towards the working foot (i.e. *battements tendus* side *passé devant; glissades* and *sissonnes dessus*). Or it can be said – the head usually turns towards the foot closing in front (figure 50).

(b) *The head when travelling backwards*

When travelling backwards the head usually INCLINES towards the supporting foot (i.e. *battements tendus* side *passé derrière; glissades* and *sissonnes dessous*) (figure 51).

(c) *The head in Ronds de jambe à terre*

The above rules should be used during *ronds de jambe à terre*.

46

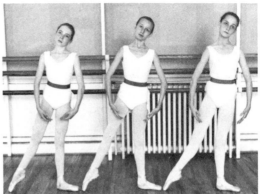

Figure 50. The head TURNS towards the working foot when coming forward.

Figure 51. The head INCLINES towards the supporting foot when going backwards. Centre girl's weight is not fully over supporting leg. The girl on the right has her arms a little wide.

En dehors. The head slightly inclines and glances over the supporting leg as the working foot stretches to *pointe tendue devant;* straightens when the leg moves to the side, and then inclines over the supporting leg as the working leg reaches the back. It can also (as in figure 54) slightly turn towards the audience (figures 52, 53 and 54).

En dedans. The head inclines over the supporting leg as the working foot stretches to *pointe tendue derrière,* straightens and then inclines and glances at the working foot as it reaches the front.

A good rule to follow when using the inclinations of the head and holding the arms in third or fourth position (R.A.D.) is to ensure that during the early stages of training the head inclines over the supporting leg if the working leg is raised in front or behind, and is either bent or straight, the arm on the same side of the body being raised in front or over the head, because all three things, i.e. head, arm and leg, should not be balanced on the same side.

However, if the working leg is raised to the side, or more importantly *écarté devant,* an exception is made to this rule because the head is TURNED towards the raised leg and not INCLINED.

(d) *The use of the head in épaulements*

Today, each school uses the nine points of the square to which each movement should be directed. In the old French (i.e. Bournonville and his pupil Johannson) and Italian schools (i.e. Blasis) this meant that whereas the hips and shoulders faced the same plane and were directed towards one of the nine points of the square, the dancer's head had to be turned towards the audience (or front), except in *écarté devant* or *derrière,* when the head was turned sideways towards the corner nearest the audience. This gave rise to the slight turn of the body still used in certain movements of the Russian school. This convention of always

Figure 52. The head slightly inclines and glances over the supporting foot, *pointe devant*. The girl on the right has slightly foreshortened her leg into the hip socket.

Figure 53. Straightens when *à la seconde*.

Figure 54. Or slightly turns towards audience when *pointe derrière*.

turning the head towards the audience is valuable at the beginning of training, but the child must be taught that in modern choregraphy, any one of the nine points can be used as a front, as this gives greater freedom to the head and widens the field through which the total line of the dance can flow (figures 55–59).

Figures 55–59. The épaulements.

Figure 55. FRONT: *pointe tendue devant: croisé, de face, effacé.*

Figure 56. BACK: *pointe tendue derrière: croisé, de face, effacé.*

Although each school refers to the eight points of a square, in reality there are nine because there are three aspects of each direction. Working with right foot *pointe tendue* and the dancer facing the audience, these nine directions are:
  Devant; De face, croisé and *éffacé* (figure 55).
  Derrière; De face, croisé and *éffacé* (figure 56).
  Side; De face, écarté devant and *écarté derrière* (figure 57).
The misconception arose because when the analysis of the eight points was first made, it was found too difficult musically to phrase an exercise with a sequence of nine movements.

Figure 57. SIDE: *pointe tendue écarté devant, de côté, écarté derrière.*

Figure 58. Same as *55*, but girls have new front.

Figure 59. Each girl has new front.

(e) *The use of the head en place and when travelling*

A clear distinction must be made between the use of the head when the dancer poses *en place* and when travelling.

En Place: The head should be placed in the correct position and alignment (i.e. as in the above) immediately before the dancer arrives in the pose, because the eyes should always indicate the line and position to be taken, and therefore should slightly anticipate the movement and remain absolutely still when the position or pose is taken.

Travelling: The eyes and head indicate the direction to be travelled and must be trained not only to anticipate that direction, but also to some extent indicate the rise and fall of the movement (if such exists). e.g. if a *grand jeté en avant* is to soar up and over, the head and eyes lead the movement upwards before the leap, but if it is a modern *jeté développé*, the eyes project the line forwards and not so high.

Pirouettes: The only exception to the above rules is the head in *pirouettes*. In all early training the child must be taught to turn the head freely from side to side independently of the body, particularly of the shoulders so that when a single *pirouette* is attempted, the eyes exactly focus the spot at which they will begin and finish their turn. The child then keeps the eyes focussed at that spot as the turn begins and until no further movement is possible. At that moment it immediately turns its head to the front and refocusses the original spot.

At a later stage when *pirouettes* have to be finished facing another front, there are two ways of finding this new spot:

(a) The eyes focus the new front, just AFTER the turn begins. This was advocated by Vaganova and Messerer, who believed that the speed and number of turns required the eyes to find the new front as quickly as possible before any sense of direction was lost.

(b) The eyes focus their "spot" as the turn begins, but immediately re-focus the front or audience and continue facing the front, only finding the new "spot" as the turn finishes (Cecchetti).

However, the head must never be turned to the new "spot" with the preparation. It must turn AFTER the turn begins.

4. CONVENTIONAL MOVEMENTS OF THE ARMS

The conventional uses of the arms are to help maintain the dancer's equilibrium, give co-ordination between body and limbs and some continuity of line in the early stages of training. It was for this reason that in classwork of the old French and Italian schools the arms were continually being passed through or held in first position (R.A.D.). In other words the arms moved into this position whenever there was a transfer of weight from one foot to the other through one of the closed positions, thus ensuring the stability of the body at each change, because the weight was equally distributed over both feet at this moment and the arms were equally balanced. Further, the arms were always opened or balanced in second position whenever the feet were opened and held or passed through second position. Similarly, the arms were moved in third or fourth position whenever the feet were held or passed through fourth position; e.g. as they do in a conventional performance of a *pas de basque* (figures 97–101).

(a) *Arms when working en place at the barre*

The conventional *ports de bras* in which the arm comes from *bras bas* then moves to first or fifth position and opens to second position should precede each exercise at the barre, except in those where the working arm is slightly lifted sideways with an intake of breath before the leg (or legs) begin to move. By using such a preparation children become used to following the proper line (see p. 79.)

It should always be remembered that in pure classical dance the fingertips never meet at or touch the centre line of the body. In first or fifth position (R.A.D.) they are about four inches apart for girls and the width of the forehead apart for boys. Therefore it cannot be emphasized strongly enough that the arm, when rounded or straight in *arabesque*, must never narrow the chest and shoulder because the space between arm and body should always be seen to give room to the dancer to move calmly and generously (see p. 135).

(b) *Arms when working en place in the centre*

When the child leaves the barre to work in the centre, it is essential to use the conventional *ports de bras* so that they help to balance the body, therefore the child must again ensure that neither arm crosses the centre line of balance and begin to understand how the counter pull of forces helps to keep the body upright.

The counter pull of forces means bringing the natural law of opposition into full use, e.g. as in *grands battements*, *développés* or *relevés en croix*. If the left leg is raised in front the arms move from first into an open fourth position with right arm curved over the head and left in second; the right arm then descends to first position as the left moves to *bras bas* and returns to first simultaneously with the right; then as the left leg is raised to side, the arms again move to an open fourth, but the left arm moves over the head and the right opens to second position, thus helping to counter-balance the raised leg; once again the arms describe the *ports de bras* as above and return to first position, but as the left leg is raised behind:

I. both arms can open to second position equally balancing the body;

or

II. the right arm can stretch outwards to side, or (at a later stage) downwards and backwards as the left arm moves forwards, thus both arms move into an *arabesque* line. This last should not be attempted until the child is able to keep shoulders and hips facing the same plane and can lower and turn the backwards moving arm in its socket so that the shoulder does not move (figures 60–62).

(c) *The arms when travelling sideways or écarté*

To begin a step travelling sideways or *écarté*, the same arm as foot in front should be curved in front of the body, the other held sideways in second (i.e. third position) and be replaced there at the finish of each step such as *glissades*, *assemblés* and *sissonnes fermées*. Thus if the feet do not change relationship, the

Figures 60–62. The counter pull of forces.

Figure 60. En avant.

Figure 61. A la seconde. The muscles are still not strong enough to keep the hips level at this height.

Figure 62. En arabesque (during the first stage of training).

same arm as foot in front is placed in front of the body during the preparation, opens to second as the step proceeds and curves in front of the body as the feet close in fifth position. But if the feet change their relationship, then the arms will also change.

7

THE DEVELOPMENT OF CHILDREN WITH
YOUTHFUL SKELETAL AGE

A CHILD of youthful skeletal age is described by Professor Tanner of the Institute of Child Health as one whose physique is insufficiently mature at the age of 10–11, when he is asked by the Royal Ballet School to predict its ultimate height. In other words the child's bones, muscles and nerves have not matured as fast as those in other children of this age. It is not easy to recognise such a child at a glance and teachers should accept this as a natural phenomenon and not as maladjustment. Nevertheless it is useful to give some explanation as such children do have certain difficulties which a teacher may think are faults, but which arise from their lack of muscle tone and powers of co-ordination.

1. The development of an adequate dance technique in any child with youthful skeletal age is difficult to predict because such children pose problems not met with elsewhere. Not only are their bones delayed, but the whole development of the child, and this presumably means control from brain over muscles and nerves too. Hence Professor Tanner is inclined to believe that their system of proprioceptive nerves is not adequately developed (see below), or those parts of their brain dealing with movement do not yet function efficiently. This may well be a reason why such children are unable to "feel" a movement through their limbs and body to their extremities. Moreover there is always some lack of co-ordination, which is most apparent in the regions of ankle, thighs, wrists, shoulders and neck.

N.B. The proprioceptive nerves are those which transmit signs from the periphery to the brain through the full length of limbs and body saying where things are, thus indicating the shape the movement must take, the relationship of each part to the whole and the relationship of each part to another (e.g. the distance and stretch between hip and toe, or the stretch between little finger and thumb).

As such children grow and assimilate the classical technique, girls acquire greater control over the upper half of the body (i.e. from the waist upwards) whilst the boys acquire greater control over the lower half, except from the ankle downwards. From there the boys still continue to lack strength and sensitivity, although the rest of their legs are far from adequately controlled.

This happens because girls do develop in general earlier than boys and hence it should be expected that at the same chronological age their control of their muscles should be better. They do possibly have the same degree of control in the pelvis and hips as boys, but because this area is wider in girls than in boys, it is just more difficult to handle. As the girls have to move heavier weights in this area, they really need stronger muscles, and these THEY DO NOT HAVE as the extra size of the pelvis is largely due to bones and fat. Such details are independent of training as they are natural phenomena. All that can be done is to ensure that neither boy nor girl is over-stretched at the difficult transition period of development.

2. Children with youthful skeletal age usually lack muscle tone in every way and there is a strong difference between girls and boys. Boys seem unable to stretch outwards from the centre of their chest to their finger-tips, have little or no strong movement from their shoulder-blades, breathe rather shallowly because they are unable to "feel" how their intercostal muscles work, and usually hold their heads as if firmly "stuck" on their shoulders, always finding it difficult to use their heads independently of their neck and body.

Girls on the other hand are usually able to "feel" this stretch and the use of the intercostal and other muscles, but nearly always lack control in the region of the pelvis and hip-joints. (see 4).

3. Children's feet usually stop growing before the rest of their bodies, but feet differ from child to child rather independently of other parts of the body (except hands) so that there are great differences in the proportion height to foot length. The difference in size and relationship of foot to height seems to affect the child with youthful skeletal age more than the average child.

Those who have large feet for their size seem to acquire strength to balance and jump fairly easily, but lose this ability if they start to grow rapidly and the feet do not grow similarly. But those who have an extra long big toe only begin to "feel" how to balance and jump after the other toes begin to stretch out.

Similarly those children whose feet are small for their height have the utmost difficulty in balancing and jumping. Such children must be trained very early to keep their weight well forwards over the three points of balance of their feet and MUST BE HELPED to "feel" the stretch upwards from the waist to a far greater extent than the normal child. They must NOT RISE HIGHER THAN *demi-pointe*. Also far greater attention must be paid to the free use of the head, although results of this care are frequently not evident for some two or three years of regular training.

N.B. It is still not known at what age the child with youthful skeletal age acquires full control over his or her body, or "feels" the movement really flowing throughout their limbs. Usually they are two-three years behind, and so one would expect that they would have the usual degree of control two–three years later than the normal child. But it would seem that the final details of "feeling" a dance movement to its ultimate extent varies considerably, it may take seven years or over.

4. Because girls with youthful skeletal age tend to develop before they can "feel" movement flowing through the torso, they must be made to understand how to use the lower intercostal muscles to lift the rib-cage. On no account should they be allowed to lift the bust alone by merely protruding and raising

the breast-bone, because this pushes the shoulders back and exaggerates the arched back, which is – in its turn – generally weak or lacks muscle tone. They should also be taught at this stage to pull the legs strongly away from the hips by using exercises which require strong pressure into and out of the floor.

Another very important point to stress when teaching those with growth problems is always to see that they focus their eyes at the proper level so that the head is held correctly at all times. It so often happens, even with children growing gradually, that having established the right "spot" to focus when first starting work at the barre they continue to focus that same "spot" regardless of increasing height. This must be prevented at all times, otherwise chins can sink, chest and shoulders tense and be drawn inwards instead of being held freely upwards and outwards away from the spine. It is particularly important for boys, who have to acquire breadth and strength of stance and movement across this area as well as the ability to hold the spine and head fully erect. This is absolutely necessary even though their muscles may not yet be strong or controlled enough to maintain this stance throughout every exercise.

By insisting on the correct focus of the eyes and the free carriage of the head both growing boys and girls will learn how to cope more easily with their increasing weight, height and breadth. The boys should be encouraged to concentrate more on the control over legs and arms (see Chapter 4). This gives them greater breadth and strength of movement, particularly in those muscles emanating from the spine and head which help to control the action of the arms, and their breathing. Girls should concentrate more on their bodies, particularly the muscles within the pelvis, the inner and outer thighs and stomach. They must be taught to pull the "tail" downwards, the legs outwards in the hip-joints and the stomach muscles used in breathing upwards. Breathing muscles, in both boys and girls, emanate upwards from the spine and downwards from the head.

On no account must the ribs be lifted too high in either boy or girl. Admittedly, it is difficult to make them feel how this is done. But it should be tried. It is as if the lowest ribs are being raised upwards from underneath by a pull from the hip-joints through the waist to the diaphragm. The ribs can then be allowed to expand outwards and inwards whilst breathing. This prevents the diaphragm from bulging forwards. It is therefore important that correct breathing is practised at all times, particularly by those of youthful skeletal age (see Chapter 9).

8

WORK DURING THE GIRL'S MONTHLY PERIODS

Iᴛ ɪs perhaps worth noting that at their first menstruation and at any similar period thereafter every Soviet girl no matter who they are or what work they do can claim three days rest. As a rule most do claim that right. The girls in all Soviet Ballet schools therefore have the same privilege. But it rather depends upon the individual child. In general, teachers are agreed that during the girl's first year of regular menstruation they should not be expected to dance during the first and second days but should attend half a class on the third, unless there is any pain, discomfort or some abnormality. After that the girl should dance normally.

But very much depends on the individual. Recently it has been found that certain girls coming from modern outwards-looking homes and brought up on a modern diet, suffer so little that these are encouraged to rest only on the first day during the first year of menstruation and after this allowed to dance right through. However it should be born in mind that girls dancing through their periods are more prone to accidents as they are always less controlled. Because of this and the decision to allow girls to work during menstruation it is useful to observe the following in order to strengthen the abdominal, buttock and back muscles during early training.

1. It is important during the first year of training to concentrate on the stomach muscles which must always be kept in a state of tonicity, i.e. ᴘᴜʟʟᴇᴅ-ᴜᴘ (not in) and always ready to play their proper part in helping buttocks to pull inwards, spine downwards and rib-cage upwards. On no account must breathing be too deep, nor too shallow, i.e. the breath should not enter the stomach nor the lungs be over-filled at the top. The rib-cage and diaphragm must learn to play a proper part (see pp. 61–62).

2. During the second year, proper training of the back should begin, i.e. the spine must always be kept straight and pulled downwards from the waist to the "tail" with further concentration on the pulling inwards of the buttock muscles, whilst keeping the stomach flat. There must be no "tucking in" of the tail and therefore no contraction of the stomach muscles or "rock" of the spine.

But during the same period some degree of flexibility must be allowed from the waist upwards, always keeping the shoulders level and pulled outwards, with the arms in front of the shoulders so that even in a sideways bend, the shoulders retain their correct relationship with the spine (i.e. at right angles). Great emphasis should be made on keeping the weight forwards over the balls of the feet, particularly when the girl begins to develop bust and buttocks (see pp. 33–36).

3. During the third year emphasis should be placed on giving full flexibility to the spine by adding body movements to the side, front and back in most *ports de bras* and in simple adagios, particularly at the barre.

N.B. It is during such exercises that a girl having her period should not be encouraged to stretch too much. She should rather be encouraged TO DANCE the movement than execute it technically and correctly. This is done so that natural dance qualities such as line and musicality are retained because the period is – at this point – an indication of growing maturity, therefore the body must become more expressive (figures 63–67).

During the fourth year body movements should be co-ordinated in any appropriate exercise which is – at this stage – comparatively simple, but the *enchaînements* should be longer in order to build up stamina.

Figures 63–67. Teenagers dancing.

Figure 63. Développé en avant.

Figure 64. Port de bras.

Figure 65. Each boy takes two girls.

Figure 66. The promenade begins.

Figure 67. Boy in *cabriole*.

9

THE TRAINING OF THE BACK AND BREATHING

THE classical dancer, both boy and girl achieve the best results when the spine has been straightened to its fullest extent. But so often when this happens the spine is stiffened and becomes strained because its three natural curves have been eliminated and deprived of their true function. These three natural curves act as shock-absorbers, therefore they must be trained to respond at all times to the total movement of the body. This is why the child, particularly the girl, should be taught to keep the upper half of the torso as flexible as possible whilst maintaining the pure classical stance. In order to do this the spine must be trained to bend in three places without disturbing the true centre of balance which every dancer must acquire if he or she is to maintain the turn-out, the preparation and landing from any jump, *pirouette*, pose, etc.

The three places are from the waist upwards:–

1. *The First Bend* takes place from the head alone. It moves freely backwards on top of the spine quite independently of the neck muscles, the shoulders being held still and relaxed. The chin is quietly directed upwards to the ceiling without any poke forwards.

2. *The Second Bend* takes place as the shoulder-blades are slid downwards and slightly inwards towards the spine at the same time as the ribs are lifted upwards with an intake of breath in order to give freedom at the waist-line.

3. *The Third Bend* is achieved by increasing the curve already begun by curving the cervical spine still further and thus increasing the lift of the ribs and the bending back of the head and shoulders. An important item to notice is that once the head and shoulders reach their fullest extension in the second bend, they remain practically still so that the muscles of stomach and diaphragm can be stretched upwards to their limit. If this lifting of the ribs and their extension sideways are performed correctly, there should be no arching of the back and thus no "rocking" of the pelvis when the ultimate extent of the bend is reached. In other words, the lower half of the back retains its position because it does not move.

I. PRELIMINARY EXERCISE FOR THE BACK BEND IN THREE MOVEMENTS

1. *Head Bend*

Stand naturally at the barre, chin in – but not pressed in – feet in easy first; pubic bones or stomach pressed lightly on the barre; hold with both hands wherever comfortable and where the child is able to maintain the starting position from the waist downwards.

Bend head backwards, freeing chin and directing it towards the ceiling AFTER the head has started to move. Curve head backwards as far as possible without moving shoulder or neck muscles.

On returning to the upright position the chin should fall back correctly into place, if the spine is pulled straight (figure 68).

The back bend.

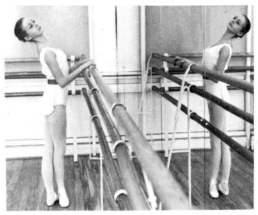

Figure 68. Bend of the head.   *Figure 69*. Breathe in for cervical spine bend.

2. *Shoulder Bend*

Commencing with the head back as above and slightly inclined to left or right, push upwards from the lower frontal ribs. It is useful to suggest that this is easier if the child breathes in (figure 69).

Slide the shoulder-blades slightly downwards and inwards to the spine. (The shoulders are pressed DOWN and not back.) The chest must NOT be protruded, it moves upwards only.

Flex the upper, or cervical spine, try to curve the shoulders backwards and downwards. The stomach must be kept absolutely still and lightly pressed to the barre.

3. *Waist Bend*

Starting with the shoulders curved backwards, stretch still further upwards from the lower ribs and curve the body further by directing the shoulders backwards.

Curve the head a little further backwards and flex or curve the spine from ABOVE the waist only. On no account let the head drop backwards (figure 70).

The entire movement is upwards and backwards in a curve. The pelvis must be kept absolutely still throughout in order to maintain balance, the feet must grip the floor, the leg muscles must be pulled up, but the back moves freely from the waist upwards.

It will be found that all exercises relating to the stretching and bending of the back will be made easier if the child is taught to breathe correctly and at the right moment. That is, when a physical effort has to be made to achieve some movement by bringing the accessory respiratory muscles into play together with the usual muscles of respiration.

Figure 70. Stretch further upwards and over.

Breathing is controlled by the respiratory centre in the brain. When this centre is stimulated the master nerves which supply the respiratory muscles cause them to contract. The muscles of respiration are the diaphragm and inter-costals, and the contraction of these muscles increases the lung space within the chest wall and the lungs can fill with air. Inspiration is an active process, that is, the muscles are contracted. Expiration is a passive process; that is, there is a recoil of the elastic tissue of the lungs and the air space diminishes once again.

When respiration is increased, for example in exercise (dancing) the accessory respiratory muscles are also used. All the chief accessory muscles are attached to the cervical (neck) region of the spinal column or to the skull, and are the sterno-mastoid, scalene and the upper part of the trapezius muscles. If the shoulder is fixed by holding on to something, e.g. the barre, the pectorals are also used to assist breathing. Therefore, if the dancer is to maintain the air-space – i.e. the "gap" throughout any exercise away from the barre, then the pectorals are used more than in normal breathing. Note how much easier it is to lift the rib-cage from underneath if the child breathes in, and how much easier to slide the shoulder-blades down the spine if the ribs are expanded sideways and the diaphragm kept flat.

2. ANALYSIS OF BREATHING FOR DANCERS

The dancer must breathe in with the stomach muscles in a state of tonicity, i.e. the stomach must not be pulled in, nor stuck out. It must be held comfortably upwards by the strong pull of the abdominal muscles.

If a return is made to the beginning of the shoulder bend above, i.e. lifting of the lower ribs away from the waist, but with the head ERECT, the body is in the correct position for dancing and breathing (see p. 9).

N.B. There is now a much larger "gap" between the top of the thighs and the bottom of the ribs, the diaphragm is free to move, the stomach is held flat but NOT CONTRACTED.

1. It is essential that a dancer never breathes with a rigid chest. It must be mobile and held calmly.

2. The abdomen must be quite still, neither relaxed nor contracted, i.e. in a state of tonicity.

3. The ribs can now be lifted upwards and simultaneously expanded sideways and outwards; or relaxed downwards and contracted inwards by the action of the intercostal and accessory respiratory muscles and diaphragm as the child breathes out.

4. The chest can be expanded sideways and forwards and backwards by the movement of the sternum upwards.

3. PREPARATION FOR BREATHING EXERCISES

1. Stand correctly with palms of hands upon sides of chest on a level with the bottom of the breast-bone. Breathe in and see how far the fingers can be pressed apart by: (a) a small breath; (b) a larger breath; (c) a very deep breath.

N.B. The breath should be directed towards the place indicated by the hands.

2. With one hand pressed on the abdominal wall, so that it does not move at all, and the other hand lightly held on the diaphragm, breathe in, consciously using the diaphragm, making it swell outwards with the inhalation and fall inwards with the expiration.

N.B. This is the natural process, but the child must be conscious of this as it is the action of the diaphragm contracting that maintains the "gap" i.e. allows the chest to remain firmly raised and the ribs to function easily.

4. PRELIMINARY EXERCISE FOR CORRECT BREATHING FOR DANCERS

A combination of the above two examples is the correct breathing method for dancers.

1. Breathe in, allowing the chest to expand sideways and the diaphragm to swell easily, but not overfill (figures 71a and b).

2. Breathe out allowing the diaphragm to contract to support the chest (figures 72a and b).

N.B. Be sure that the "gap" is maintained.

Counting for breathing exercises should be varied, sometimes slowly, sometimes quickly, but always commence evenly.

Later, when the child has fully grasped the correct method of breathing, practice taking in a quick breath (1); hold and exhale (2); take in a long breath

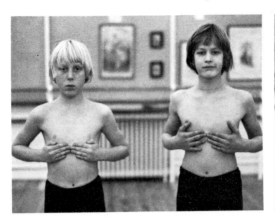 

Figure 71. (a) Relax and exhale, front view.
(b) Relax and exhale, back view. Arms down to
show shoulder lines.

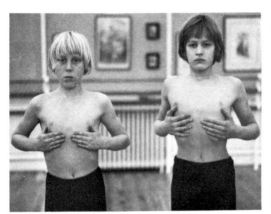 

Figure 72. Breathe in and expand chest, lifting rib-cage and
slimming waist. (a) front view; (b) back view.

(taking 4 beats); exhale (also taking 4 beats). It is advisable, from time to time, to change to other variations on this theme.

Breathing with Pliés

The best moment to introduce correct breathing is with the *pliés* during the first lessons and at the beginning of the normal class.

Exercise 1. BASIC FORM AND TIMING OF *DEMI-* AND FULL *PLIÉS*
(see also p. 80)

Use eight bars of slow waltz (girls) or four bars of slow 4/4 (counted in beats for boys). Perform in first, second and third or fifth positions, either holding the barre with both or one hand only, in which case there must be a gentle movement of the working arm. This is very valuable in helping children to understand the action of the diaphragm and rib-cage.

Bars

1–2. Commence in first position, working arm softly rounded (*bras bas*) and breathe in as the arm is pressed gently outwards from the body. At the same time relax the knees outwards and downwards keeping them over the toe line of the turned-out feet, back erect so that the "tail" appears to be pulled down towards and over the heels. There must be no other movement, i.e. the extent of the *demi-plié* has been reached (figure 40 and p. 80).

3–4. Breathe out and as the knees straighten, allow the arm to close softly to *bras bas*.

5–8. Repeat *demi-plié* as above.

Bars

1–2. Breathe in slowly and just after 3, raise heels gradually and relax knees into full *plié* on 4; begin to breathe out slowly and rise so that just after 5, the heels are replaced and pushed into the floor. During 6–7–8, straighten the knees. During the full *plié* the arm can either move more slowly outwards and inwards as before, or can complete a normal *ports de bras* (see p. 79). The breath regulates the duration of the *plié*.

N.B. After the heels have left the floor for the full *plié* the position of the knees in relationship to the spine, thighs and heels must not change so that the weight is held over the whole foot with the knee directly in a line with the toes. The rounded arm must not be dropped below the spot at which it was held in *bras bas* when the exercise began.

BREATHING AND RISING

As the dancer does not always make a downwards effort, and as the effort is not always made in the same set of muscles, it is also valuable to combine *pliés* with a rise to *demi-pointe* and an intake of breath, especially in those cases where a rise or *relevé* is followed by a *ports de bras*.

Exercise 2. *PLIÉS* FINISHING IN *PORTS DE BRAS*

Repeat *plié* exercise as above in first position and with an intake and exhalation of breath, rise on *demi-pointe* instead of using second *demi-plié*, using the same arm movement. After the full *plié*, continue stretching upwards on to *demi-pointe*, raising arm to fifth position and taking another eight bars or beats:—

Bars

1–4. Breathe in, bending as far forwards as possible from the "hinge" keeping the head in the same line as the fully straightened spine and without allowing the "gap" to close (figure 13).

5–8. Recover very slowly, breathing out.

Repeat *plié* exercise in second position, using rise instead of second *demi-plié*. After full *plié*, rise to *demi-pointe* raising arm first to fifth position.

Bars

1–4. Breathe in and bend sideways towards the barre. It is important to feel the lift of the rib-cage before the sideways bend. The shoulders must be

The sideways bend.

Figure 73. Shoulders remain in correct relationship to spine.

kept in their correct relationship to the spine (i.e. at right angles, figure 73).

5–8. Recover very slowly breathing out.

Repeat *plié* exercise in third or fifth position, rise to *demi-pointe*, leaving arm in second position.

Bars

1–4. Softly bend body forwards as far as possible, dropping arm to *bras bas*, (see note, p. 79 and figures 74–76). Breathing in.

5–8. Slowly straighten, breathing out. Once the erect position is reached, breathe in again and continue into the three bends of the preliminary back bend (see p. 60), either opening arm to second position, leaving it in first (this is very helpful to the youngest children), or raising it to fifth position.

N.B. The *ports de bras* can be used without a rise to *demi-pointe*. But the added stretch of the feet and legs gives greater extension to the body and more fullness to the movement.

Figures 74–76. The forwards bend.

Figure 74. Lift upwards and begin to incline graciously.

Figure 75. Bend further as if to pick up something.

Figure 76. A complete relaxation, but with leg muscles and those in stomach and pelvis completely under control.

BREATHING AND THE MAINTENANCE OF THE "GAP"

By straightening the spine and lifting the lower ribs the dancer gains greater freedom of movement in the waist line, and the legs can move more freely within the hip socket because the weight is carried more through the centre line of the body. At the same time the upper half of the body can also move more freely when required. Exercises should be given to make children understand how to maintain the "Gap" between the top of the thighs and the lower ribs as well as the placing of the limbs and head in relationship to the central line of balance running through the spine. Movements studied during the first years of training should be so arranged that the line is continually being transferred through the central point from one leg to another, and from one pose to another (figures 27–28).

BREATHING IN ALL ADAGIOS

Breathing will help to lengthen the period of balance when the working leg is held or moved from one pose to another. A proper phrasing of the breath adds fullness to the movement, as can be demonstrated by practising such exercises as those for *développés* in three stages or *ronds de jambe à terre* with *ports de bras* (see p. 94).

BREATHING AND PIROUETTES

A well controlled intake of breath as the dancer rises from the preparation on to *demi-* or full *pointe* and begins to turn, lend greater stability to every type of *pirouette* and particularly so at a later stage when the boy and girl commence double work and supported *pirouettes*. The intake of breath should be so timed that it continues throughout the turn, is held momentarily as the turn finishes on the supporting leg and is exhaled as the working foot closes in some position or is held in some pose (see p. 108).

BREATHING AND JUMPING

Finally breathing must be used to help all types of jumps, particularly all forms of *Grand Elevation* where the correct timing of the intake must coincide with the push into and out of the floor with the *demi-plié;* the holding of breath with the calm hold of the entire body in the requisite pose as it moves through the air. The breath is then exhaled JUST AFTER the supporting foot descends into *fondu* (or both feet into *demi-plié*).

It is because steps of grand elevation are so varied in quality, and require such different types of preparation and accenting, if each step is to be performed correctly and lightly, that all preparatory work on this type of movement should be practised at the barre and be as varied as possible (see p. 115).

USE OF THE SHOULDERS

It is not enough to give the back flexibility if the arms do not move freely within the shoulder-sockets to play their full part in certain movements. Every child should learn to "feel" the pressure of the air as they draw their arms inwards and outwards, or upwards and downwards. They must also learn to raise their arms softly and directly upwards into second position without any twist of the upper arm. There is also the subtle movement to be studied early when the arm, moving backwards into an *arabesque* line from first position or open fourth must lower and turn slightly in its socket as it comes towards and passes beyond the shoulder joint, if the shoulders are to remain square to their front and not be distorted in any way, as will surely happen if the child attempts to move the arm through second position.

Stand correctly, arms hanging relaxed to the sides and WITHOUT ALTERING the shoulder line or level, roll the shoulders outwards and backwards towards the spine at the same moment as inhaling, thus expanding the chest. Hold breath for a moment, then exhale, rolling the shoulders as far forwards as possible, at the same time lower the chest very slightly.

This exercise is most valuable when co-ordinated with the classical walk (see p. 140).

10

THE DEVELOPMENT OF A PROPER TURN-OUT

THE classical dancer requires the legs to be fully turned-out from the hip-joints if his or her movements are to achieve the true line. It is essential to help the child accomplish the correct turn-out without unnecessary strain or forcing which so easily leads to trouble later in the region of the groin. The so-called "FROG" exercises lying or sitting on the floor should be practised from the first days of training. If these are performed correctly they help children to understand the feel of the straight back, the necessary pull on the buttock muscles which gives strength to every leg movement, the need to expand the chest in such a way that the shoulders slide almost imperceptibly down the spine, and the arms to open freely as the child breathes fully and deeply.

1. "FROGS" ON THE FLOOR TO HELP THE TURN-OUT

1. The child lies on the floor, legs straight, body relaxed with shoulders down so that the whole spine is flat on the floor and perfectly straight. (Few children seem able to "feel" the straight line through the body when they first attempt this.)

2. From this position and without using any other movement the arms should be raised upwards to a well-rounded first position (i.e. exactly opposite the diaphragm, no higher) and opened, still rounded into second position so that the chest can be felt to open outwards without any movement of the torso, because the whole spine lies along the floor. The arms must now be in a true second position, i.e. sloping downwards from the shoulders. The head is now turned from side to side so that the child can "feel" this turning without tilting or poking the head. (N.B. Girls must not have a bun at the nape of the neck.)

3. The child then relaxes the arms and lets them fall softly outstretched at the side and turns the legs outwards at the hip-joints with toes pointed, heels just off the floor and knees absolutely straight. (This is to eliminate any sign of "sickle".) In some cases where the calf is large, the feet may leave the floor if the knees are pulled up tightly. This is not a fault and should not be corrected as it is due mainly to the difference in size of foot (turned-out) and calf.

4. From the above position the child must now pull the knees upwards and outwards, keeping outside of legs as long as possible on the floor with the spine still touching and straight, shoulders down. (There should be some pull on the buttock muscles as this is done, in order to pull the spine a little straighter.)

Once this position has been achieved by conscious effort, the child should then relax in "Frogs" and stay for as long as ten minutes. Five minutes is considered the minimum necessary at the beginning of training. The entire spine must be flat throughout this relaxation (figures 77–80).

Figures 77–80. Frogs.

Figure 77. Lie flat, legs straight, arms in first position.

Figure 78. Turn legs out from thighs, open arms to second position.

2. "FROGS" AGAINST THE WALL TO HELP TURN-OUT AND THE NEED TO MAINTAIN A STRAIGHT SPINE WITH FREEDOM OF THE HEAD

1. The child sits absolutely flat against a wall, legs stretched straight out in front so that they are at an angle of 90° to the body (i.e. the pelvis and legs are at right angles to each other). This position is very difficult for those with tight

Figure 79. Draw toes up, opening knees as far as possible. (N.B. Arms have been lifted to show possible stretch of body.)

Figure 80. Lie relaxed in "frogs" for at least five minutes.

ham-strings, but by making an effort such children become aware of their some-what restricted movement and are made more conscious of the need to stretch the spine to its fullest extent by using all the muscles of buttocks, abdomen, waist and pelvis to attain greater flexibility. Such children may find it easier at first to place their hands on the floor by their sides. This gives them a lever to help maintain a straight back, the shoulders must not be raised but kept open and relaxed as far as possible.

2. Once in this position, the head should be turned freely from side to side with no other movement appearing elsewhere at all.

3. With legs straight, toes should now be turned up and down several times with calves pressed lightly on the floor, thus ensuring the knees are kept straight.

72

Figure 81. To show difference in height between two boys of roughly same age.

Figure 82. To show ability of boy to pull spine to straightest.

By so doing the movement can be felt to run through the centre of the leg to the foot.

4. Now turn-out the legs from the hip-joint only and then inwards, repeating this rotation several times with the legs and feet fully stretched. Later, with toes fully pointed, gradually draw the knees upwards, heels just off the floor, toes pressing lightly on the ground and keeping the knees as widely opened as possible until the same "Frogs" position has been reached which was first felt when lying flat. The toes should be touching, but not necessarily the heels, although this is desirable if it does not lead to a "sickled" foot. This position should ensure that the child feels the full length of the spine from "tail" to head as well as the "hinge" of the hip-joint. (*N.B.* The hands should not rest on the floor in this position. Those with tight ham-strings may use them as it is practically impossible for such a child to sit thus without some leverage from the arms, figures 81, 82.)

73

5. A further extension to this part of "Frogs" can be used with very great care by those children whose ham-strings are normal. These can usually sit absolutely erect with their legs straight out in front of their bodies and bend forwards from the "hinge" without any curve of the back. But this is dangerous if insisted upon for those with tight ham-strings. In such cases it is better to cultivate the important straight forwards bend of the body from the "hinge" standing with either one or two hands on the barre and attempting to keep the legs perpendicular to the floor (figures 13, 14).

3. PLIÉS AGAINST A WALL TO HELP THE TURN-OUT AND THE ERECT BACK

Whenever possible it is valuable to place children behind the barre in early lessons for *pliés* (i.e. between barre and wall) where their backs rest nearly flat on the wall with both hands held easily apart on the barre.

The usual exercise is two *demi-pliés* and one full *plié* performed twice in first position; twice in second; and twice with the right and twice with the left foot front in third and later fifth positions. The head turns first to the right and then

Figure 83. Demi-pliés behind the *barre*, showing difference in depth of *plié* between boys of roughly same height.

to the left during the *demi-pliés*, but keeps straight during the full *plié* so that the child can feel the back of the head as well as the spine flat against the wall (figure 83).

II

THE BUILD-UP OF A CLASS AND AN ANALYSIS OF THE BASIC EXERCISES IN BARRE-WORK

EVERY class should be designed to contain those basic exercises which gradually introduce the child to the various steps danced later. These exercises must cover:

1. Those which obtain correct stance, placing and turn-out, (e.g. *demi* and full *pliés, ronds de jambe*).

2. Those which give strength and flexibility to every part of the body, with particular attention to the finer details of the turn-out as it affects the action of the foot, ankle, knee and hip, (e.g. the various forms of *battements, développés* and *pointes*).

3. Those which teach the most economical, simplest and thus most direct way to perform any type of movement. No energy should be wasted but expanded on the particular purpose of each exercise, (e.g. see the correct way to perform a *retiré*, p. 107).

4. Those which teach correct breathing to ensure valuable moments of relaxation, particularly when building up to a crescendo of movement, (e.g. quickening *petits battements, ports de bras, pirouettes*).

5. Those which give some understanding of the expressive quality of each movement so that it can be seen to belong, or be a preparation for, one of the seven movements of dance, (e.g. to bend, stretch, rise, jump, glide, dart, turn).

6. Those which teach the correct timing of a movement so that the child becomes aware of the exact impetus or accent to give to each part of a movement and achieve the desired results. This requires a definition of whether the movement is away or towards the body, the pressure or "force" to be applied and where to make emphasis, (e.g. the strong push of the working foot along and off the floor before jumping in an *assemblé*, or the shoulder coming into the turn for a *pirouette*).

7. Those which quicken the ear to the call of the music, so that each movement is not only the result of the full co-ordination between every part of the body, but is also timed to suit its purpose within a step. Moreover such exercises should ensure that the child does not treat the music as a mere timekeeper. Fokine said: "It is not enough to dance on the beat. The movement must flow to, through and from the beat, pausing if necessary on the high-lighted note to make some point, perhaps in the shape of a pose, *pirouette*, beat or jump."

If these aims are to be achieved the tempo and character of each class must be calm and dignified. The most valuable class should have a theme of basic exercises which are built gradually into a dancing movement. The *Temps Lié* is a perfect example of what can be done when a lesson is properly prepared. In its simplest form it contains such basic steps as *demi-pliés*, *battements tendus*, *chassés* and *ports de bras*. But at its most elaborate can comprise *pirouettes*, many forms of *sissonnes* and other advanced work. However, such a development can only take place if proper attention is paid to the fundamental details of placing as the child transfers weight from one foot to another, whilst passing the arms through the various *ports de bras*, sinks or rises from the *fondus* and *pliés*, and above all: KEEPS THE MOVEMENT FLOWING THROUGHOUT. This flow of line is the very essence of the *Temps Lié* (literally meaning Time Linked or Steps Linked). Without it there is no demonstration of that lyrical dance quality which marks the performance of the veriest beginner as well as the greatest ballerina if both possess natural ability and musicality, those innate but elusive qualities of the natural dancer (figures 84–93, the *Temps Lié*).

Figures 84–93. Temps lié—an alternative version.

Figure 84. Prepare fifth position *croisé bras bas,* head poised.

Figure 85. Demi-plié, arms rising, heads straighten.

Figure 86. Pointe tendue devant, arms in first position.

Figure 87. Transfer weight.

76

gure 88. Pointe tendue derrière, arms both in fourth position, *ads* to audience. N.B. Child on right has over-crossed.

Figure 89. Close fifth *derriére, demi-plié,* arms move to third position, heads straighten.

gure 90. Pointe tendue side and turn head. N.B. The girls *cidentally* changed arms, this is incorrect.

Figure 91. Transfer weight, open arms to second position.

gure 92. Pointe tendue side, turn head.

Figure 93. Close fifth, ready to begin opposite side.

Every school has its own sequence of barre-work to be performed daily. It varies little from that used by the French school indicated by the Gardel Brothers (1741–1840) and Vestris (Father and Son 1760–1842), carried to Russia by Didelot (1767–1836), to Italy by Carlo Blasis (1797–1878) and Denmark by Auguste Bournonville (1805–1879) and finally by Dame Ninette de Valois to England and Georges Balanchine to America. Mention should also be made of their pupils and those of many other leading teachers who settled away from their native schools during times of war or revolution, and who gradually lost something of their own dance qualities in order to adapt their technique to the talents and physiques of their new countrymen.

The following analysis of the purpose and practice of barre-work does not cover that for advanced pupils. It hopes to cover the basic work for the younger classes upon which the whole structure of the teaching of classical dance is based.

The teacher taking the first lessons in barre-work should try to instil in his or her pupils the following basic principles which never change throughout a dancer's career.

1. The stance at the beginning and throughout each exercise must be correct: i.e. head lifted and freely poised, spine erect, "tail" pulled down, all the muscles of the legs fully stretched and the "gap" between hip-joints and lower ribs maintained. The spine only moves from the perpendicular:

(a) if the working leg is raised behind to more than an angle of 18° into some form of *arabesque*, when there must be some "tilt" of the pelvis forwards. The degree of "tilt" will depend on the height of the raised leg;

(b) if a forwards bend is required for a *ports de bras*. In this case the child must breathe in before the bend in order to lift the stomach muscles and rib-cage so that there is space at the waist line in which to move (see p. 106).

2. The weight must always be held over the supporting leg whether it is straight or *fondu*, i.e. the "tail" should be directly over the supporting heel except:

(a) when there has to be a temporary transfer of weight so that it rests equally between the two feet (e.g. Exercise 2), when the "tail" should be seen to be exactly over the space created (figure 87).

(b) when there has to be a complete transfer from one foot to the other (e.g. Exercise 12) when the transfer must be seen to pass directly from the supporting leg, through the centre between the two feet before resting firmly over the new supporting leg.

3. The straight line of both supporting and working legs must always be seen to run through the centre of the leg-bones from hip to knee, ankle and middle toes, even when knee and ankle are bent at such angles that the lower half of the working leg can move outwards from, inwards to, or upwards from the supporting leg in such exercises as *petits battements*, *battements frappés* or *fondus*, *développés*, etc. This line is most important for children having difficulty in maintaining turn-out. They should understand that no matter what degree

of turn-out is attempted (see p. 26) they must ensure that the centre of the knee, ankle and middle toes are in the same straight line indicated by the turn-out from the hip-joint. They must also ensure that the movement flows through the centre of the whole leg, i.e. from hip to knee, ankle, instep and toes IN THAT ORDER or the REVERSE, except in those movements when the action is confined to one area only, i.e. in the lower half of the leg as in *petits battements, petits ronds de jambe en l'air*, etc. The flow of movement must always be ensured by teaching that the toes must never be CLENCHED or CRAMPED.

4. The hips and shoulders must always face the same plane, i.e. square to a particular front, particularly when transferring weight from one foot to another or using one then the other foot without changing sides, e.g. two *battements tendus* front with the right foot, followed by two *battements tendus* back with the left foot, the arm moving from fifth position to *arabesque*, when all too frequently the shoulders move out of alignment.

5. The chest, shoulders and arms must always be held freely open and careful note taken of the hand on the barre. With growing children there usually has to be some little movement of the supporting hand forwards when there is any "tilt" of the pelvis to raise the leg higher than 18°. If this is not done, the elbow near the barre usually turns upwards or, occasionally, is cramped into the body thus distorting the shoulder line and/or twisting the spine in some way (see p. 34).

6. The shoulders must be kept level. Too often the shoulder on the working side is allowed to drop, particularly if the "gap" is not maintained during slow *retirés* and *développés* to the side.

7. The working arm must never cross the centre line of the body. The child should understand this imaginary line is a barrier dividing the body into two equal halves therefore, because the leg must never overcross the barrier, neither must the arm (see also p. 135).

Classical Dance demands an equally balanced symmetrical form, thus all parts of the body must be disciplined to the rules of stance and the technique of classical movements, which are reinforced by the laws of opposition, of natural *épaulement* and the conventions already set down (see p. 45).

INTRODUCTION TO THE CLASS-ROOM

It has become a practice in many schools to begin children's lessons by letting them circle the room, first walking (see Exercise 130) then running and skipping as they breathe easily in and out. It acts as a warm-up and creates a friendly atmosphere. The children finish circling at their place by the barre, bow to their teacher, turn and closing their feet in first position, perform their preparatory *ports de bras* with which most exercises should begin.

Preparatory Ports de Bras

1. Softly form the arms into a well-rounded *bras bas*, girls incline their heads slightly towards the barre, eyes glancing inside palms of hands, boys glance at hands.
2. Raise both arms to first position, children straighten heads and look forwards.

3. Open both arms, but as the nearest hand approaches the barre, glance at it, place it lightly on top, then glance at the other hand as it opens in second position.

I. *Demi and Full Pliés*

The class for every child, as for the daily warm-up of all professional dancers, begins with a series of *pliés*. It is essential to realise that the action and timing of *demi-* and full *pliés* is all important. On the correct performance of these depends the stability of the entire body at the beginning and finish of practically every kind of movement (see Exercise 1, p. 65).

Analysis of the Demi- and Full Plié

Stand in first position and with spine erect, pelvis still and "tail" pulled downwards to maintain turn-out, relax at hip-joints, knees and ankles and, as the weight of the body descends, press the heels into the floor whilst maintaining a relaxed achilles tendon. The moment when the heels must leave the floor, marks the limit of the *demi-plié*. As the weight descends still further, the heels gradually rise but the hip-joints, knees, ankles and achilles tendons remain relaxed. When the weight can descend no further because ankles, achilles, knees and hip-joints have reached the limits of relaxed movement, the full *plié* has been reached. On ascending from the full *plié*, there must be a feeling that the heels are being pulled back into the floor. Any pressure immediately causes tension in ankles, knees and achilles tendons. Once the heels are down again in the *demi-plié*, they are pressed into the floor and the entire legs then straighten to push the body upwards.

No matter how carefully the *demi-* and full *pliés* are analysed, children must realise very early that the descent and ascent of a *demi-* and/or full *plié* must be an absolutely continuous movement, whose timing can be regulated, but whose action is always the same and very smooth. NEVER SIT IN A PLIE, AND ALWAYS HAVE A FEELING OF GOING UP AS YOU GO DOWN AND VICE-VERSA.

1. The child must know exactly where the *demi-plié* finishes, particularly in the open position, i.e. at that moment when the heels must leave the floor (except in second position, which often becomes too deep). This is the strongest point of balance and leverage from which to push the body upwards into any type of jump or *pirouette*. It is the strongest and most important point where the shock-absorbing functions of the three points of the spine come fully into play, not only to help balance and propel the body into the air, but ON LANDING to keep the body still during the impact of toe then heel on the floor. It is at this moment that the nerves of the foot react sensitively to the shock and send urgent messages to the spine to keep alert and still, until a fraction of a second later when the knee followed by the hip and body can relax with the exhalation of breath (see Exercise 25).

EXERCISE 3. TO FIND THE DEPTH OF THE *DEMI-PLIÉ*

Dance to eight bars of waltz (girls) or eight bars of Mazurka (boys, who should move on second beat of bar). Commence third or fifth position.

Bars

1-2. *Battement tendu* side closing third or fifth position front.

3-4. *Battement tendu* side closing first position.

5. *Demi-plié* first position.

6. *Chassé* to second, holding *demi-plié* so that hip and shoulder levels do not change and weight is exactly centred between two feet.

7. Glide working foot back to first position, holding level of *demi-plié*.

8. Straighten knees.

When mastered, repeat moving to fourth opposite first position at front and back.

Use preparatory *ports de bras* throughout.

A little more pressure on to a *demi-plié* which all but (or does at a later stage in boy's work) brings the heels off the floor before being firmly pushed back again can increase the height of any jump, or the length of all types of *chassés*, *glissés* and *élancés* movements.

2. It is vital that the timing of all *demi-* and full *pliés* is regulated by correct breathing. At first the timing should be absolutely regular, the child taking as long to descend as to ascend. Later exercises should be given in which the timing is decided by the ultimate purpose of the exercise. In general it is possible to say:—

(a) When a *demi-plié* is a preparation for sustained movement, use a rise on to *demi-pointes* or a slow *battement tendu* before the *plié* begins. This gives a guide as to where the centre line of balance must be held after the stretch upwards from the *plié*.

EXERCISE 4. *DEMI-PLIÉ* AS PREPARATION FOR SLOW BALANCING

Dance to eight bars of slow waltz (boys and girls) or two bars very slow 4/4 (boys only). Commence third or fifth position.

Bars

1-2. *Battement tendu* side closing first position, breathing in and out. Toe must not leave the floor, heel must be pressed outwards, raised and lowered firmly. Weight must be on supporting leg.

3-4. Slow *demi-plié* in first position, breathing in and out, lifting arm softly.

5. Repeat *battement tendu* with smaller breath in and out.

6-7-8. *Demi-plié*, sink into full *plié*. Stretch out of full *plié* and on to *demi-pointe* without pausing and hold. Breathe in and exhale once during this, and take another breath to hold position. Use normal *ports de bras* but finish in fifth position, the arms moving straight upwards from first position.

(b) When *pliés* are used as a preparation for all faster movements, particularly for jumps, it is best to move downwards directly from one of the five positions, or more rarely from a quick *battement glissé* into the required position, followed by a swift relaxation into and push out of a *demi-plié*.

EXERCISE 5. *DEMI-* OR FULL *PLIÉS* AS A PREPARATION FOR QUICK JUMPS

Dance to four bars of strong 3/4, an old "A Six Temps" is ideal.

Bars

1. (i) *Demi-plié* in first, third or fifth position, jump in first, or *soubresaut* with legs fully stretched and feet closed tight together. (ii) Land in *demi-plié*, relaxing achilles tendons and knees but holding body erect, pelvis still and head erect. (iii) Straighten knees.

2. (i) *Demi-plié* and jump into second position, opening arms very slightly to sides. (ii) Land in *demi-plié*, back held strongly as before with relaxed knees and achilles. (iii) Straighten knees.

3. (i) *Demi-plié*, jump closing feet in original position. (ii) Land in *demi-plié* as above. (iii) Straighten knees.

4. (i) *Demi-plié*. (ii–iii) two quick jumps in first position, or two *changements de pieds*, or two *soubresauts*.

It is better to teach children to jump upwards in first position, *soubresauts*, *changements*, etc., before introducing any jumps that travel because the effort of lifting the body into the air from two feet with the weight equally held over both, helps to keep the body and head steady and erect as well as firmly centred over one spot. Jumps off one foot (i.e. *Temps levé*) must also be practised carefully so that the raised leg is held firmly in position with the weight centred over the supporting foot, which has to do all the work.

The effort of travelling from one spot to another often results in too much movement from the body and not enough from the legs. Moreover children often take longer than expected before learning to control the exact timing and impetus to give to a travelling movement. This can make all the difference from a jump in one place from one that travels (see Exercises 8 and 12, pp. 85 and 88).

(c) When *demi-pliés* are used as a preparation for *pirouettes* it is essential that the child knows the extent of his or her own small and large open positions and the correct placing of weight (figures 94–96).

EXERCISE 6. *DEMI-PLIÉS* AS PREPARATION FOR *PIROUETTES EN DEHORS* AND *EN DEDANS*

Dance preferably to four bars of a moderate 2/4 for *pirouettes en dehors*. Commence third or fifth position, arms *bras bas*.

Bars

1. (i) With spine fully straightened and raising arm to first position, slide whole working foot along floor sideways until it is its own length away from supporting leg, and weight is transferred firmly between two feet. (ii) *Demi-plié* closing arm into shortened first (figure 96).

Figure 94. Small and large second position.   *Figure 95.* Small and large fourth position.

Figure 96. Preparations for *pirouettes:* left, *en dedans*; right, *en dehors.*

2. (i) Straighten knees. (ii) Opening arm to second position, stretch working foot sideways to *pointe tendue* feeling inside of fully stretched leg from crutch to toes as the weight is firmly replaced over the supporting leg.

3. (i) Without moving toe, drop heel of working foot, transferring weight and *demi-plié*, again closing arm in shortened first position. (ii) Straighten knees, opening arms to second position.

4. (i) Slide foot backwards to small position, keeping whole foot on floor, weight centred between the two feet with body erect. (ii) Close feet in third or fifth position, again keeping foot flat to floor, dropping arms to *bras bas*. When this is mastered, repeat moving forwards and backwards into fourth opposite first position and later fourth opposite fifth position.

For *pirouettes en dedans* dance to four bars of 6/8, moving forwards on fifth count to carry the whole weight over to the working leg. The supporting foot is held firmly on the floor as the working knee is bent (i.e. like a small lunge. See figure 96). Continue. 1. Straighten front knee and replace weight between two feet. Last bar, close as in last bar above.

The lunging movement should also be used as a stretching movement for boys, particularly when practised sideways and backwards (figures 44–46 and Exercise 18, p. 98).

II. *Battements Tendus en Croix*

Battements tendus develop the stretch of the whole leg from hip-joint to toes, using the entire length of the leg and foot muscles in such a way that the working heel resists the pressure along the floor until the child must stretch ankle, instep and finally toes to "feel" the extended line of the leg running through the centre of the bones from hip through knee to middle toes. The movement must be done so that the body is unaffected and the weight held firmly over the supporting leg, no matter in which direction the working leg is stretched. This should be so completely free that, if needed it can be lightly lifted from the floor when at its fullest extent. But on returning it should be pressed backwards in such a way that the toes, ball of the foot and finally the heel make contact with the floor and once again take their share in supporting the weight of the body when the closed position is reached.

In performing *battements tendus* the child must first understand the "feeling" of a fully stretched leg and secondly that the "tail" is NOT TUCKED IN, because this shortens the leg in the hip socket, which usually causes the buttocks to jut out backwards as the stomach and pelvis muscles are contracted, and cannot take part in pulling the body upwards. This is particularly important when stretching to *pointe tendue derrière*. Here the weight must be firmly over and a little in front of the supporting leg. It is the exact pose that should be, but seldom is, achieved later in class following some transfer of weight over to the front foot, e.g. after a *chassé*, a *demi-contretemps* and before the final close of the feet in a *pas de basque*.

It is impossible for the child to "feel" the full extension of the leg in *battement tendu* if he or she fails to maintain the "gap" between the lower ribs and hip. The following can help as it incorporates both the necessary stretching of the body with correct breathing.

EXERCISE 7. FOR MAINTAINING THE "GAP" IN ALL POSITIONS

Dance to four bars of waltz (girls) or strong 4/4 (boys). Commence in first, third or fifth position. Perform slow *battements tendus en croix* but with a drop of the foot in all the open positions. The knees are kept straight throughout, weight is transferred equally between the two feet as the heel is dropped. The "gap" must be held and the arm raised to fifth position.

Bars

1. Breathe in and stretch leg to *pointe tendue devant* holding weight on supporting leg as in Exercise 8, see below).

2. Breathe in and drop heel in open position transferring weight equally between two feet without moving toe. (This can only happen if the pull-up is strong enough.)

3. Breathe in, raise heel, replacing weight over supporting leg.

4. Breathe out and close in first, third or fifth position. Repeat to side and back.

Because the *battement tendu* leads to many different steps it is frequently valuable to finish each movement in a *demi-plié* (see Exercise 2). Alternatively the outwards stretching movement can be accompanied by a strong bend of the supporting knee (*fondu*) which straightens again as the working foot closes in first, third or fifth position. As before there must be no displacement of weight during the *tendu*. The central line of balance must be seen to run directly through the spine from the crown of the head to the "tail", which is firmly fixed over the supporting foot. Done simply as an alternative to closing in *demi-plié*, this form of *battement tendu* opening on a *fondu* is excellent as a stretching exercise (figure 44). With further additions it is a valuable introduction to such steps as *assemblés soutenus* and *pas de basque*.

EXERCISE 8. *BATTEMENTS TENDUS* AS PREPARATION FOR *ASSEMBLÉ SOUTENU*, AND *PAS DE BASQUE*

Dance to four bars of slow mazurka for *Assemblé soutenu*. Commence third or fifth position. *Bras bas*.

Bar 1

i   Glide working foot to *pointe tendue devant* as supporting knee bends (*fondu*), raising arm to first position and inclining head to supporting side.

ii Circle working foot to *pointe tendue* side, straightening supporting knee and opening arm to second position. Straighten head.

Figures 97–101. Pas de basque.

Figure 97. Commence fifth, *bras bas*.

Figure 98. *Fondu, pointe tendue devant,* lift arms through first to third, lift head.

iii Close in third or fifth position, dropping arm *bras bas*. Repeat moving to side and back, back to side, and side to front, being careful to maintain weight fully over supporting leg, and straightening knee as the working toe circles and pauses at new *pointe tendue* position before closing.

Figure 99. Circle foot from front to side, holding *fondu,* open arms to second, turning head, before transferring weight.

Figure 100. Pass foot through first, heel just off floor, drop arms *bras bas.*

Figure 101. Transfer weight, stretching *pointe tendue derrière*: open arms through first to second. Close fifth *derrière*, as in 98, but on opposite side.

When practising for *Pas de basque,* dance to 6/8, move from front to side closing foot behind, then from back to side closing front. But hold *fondu* position until working foot closes into third or fifth position. This ensures that the circling for the *pas de basque* retains its proper breadth so that the child will travel properly to the side before stepping diagonally forwards. Note the careful timing (figures 97–101).

86

EXERCISE 9. *BATTEMENTS TENDUS* FOR GREATER TURN-OUT

Dance to a waltz. Commence first, third or fifth position and keep arm to side or hand on top of hip, this helps to keep the pelvis still and allows the child to feel exactly where the turn-out begins.

Bars
1. Stretch well turned-out leg forwards as far as possible to *pointe tendue* preserving the straight line from hip to toe.
2. Turn entire working leg inwards from hip-joint so that knee and front of foot face the ceiling. Keep toe on floor.
3. Turn leg out again to original *pointe tendue*.
4. Close first, third or fifth position.
   Repeat to side and then to back.

EXERCISE 10. *BATTEMENTS TENDUS* FOR GREATER FLEXIBILITY OF ANKLE

Dance as Exercise 9 above but instead of turning leg outwards and inwards, turn the toe straight upwards from the ANKLE ONLY, everything else remaining fully stretched. Then re-stretch ankle and instep and rest toe on floor before closing.

At a later stage some inclination of the body and head, and a slight movement of the hands and arms can lend a dance-like quality to a *battement tendu* to prepare the child for greater co-ordination. In all such exercises the timing and action are all important.

EXERCISE 11. *BATTEMENTS TENDUS* FOR GREATER CO-ORDINATION

Dance to eight bars of easy 2/4. Commence first, third or fifth position. *Bras bas.*

Bars
1. Breathe in, *battement tendu devant* opening arm through first to second position, turning hand slightly upwards and inclining head over supporting leg. Breathe out, but keep arm in second position as foot closes.
2. Breathe in, *battement tendu* side, turning hand to correct second position and head to side. Breathe out and close.
3. Breathe in and *battement tendu derrière*, slightly turning palm of hand downwards and incline head over supporting leg but glance sideways; breathe out and swing leg through first position to *pointe tendue devant* reversing movement of head and hand.
4. Breathe in, swing leg through first position to *pointe tendue derrière*, again reversing head and hand; breathe out and close both foot and arm.
   Reverse whole. Commence by raising arm to low *arabesque* but use head as above. Open arm to second position when leg moves to side.

Finally *battements tendus* are an invaluable introduction to slow *glissades* where the toes must never leave the floor, or any step where a complete change of weight must take place from one *fondu* to another *fondu* position.

EXERCISE 12. *BATTEMENTS TENDUS* AS AN INTRODUCTION TO SLOW
GLISSADES, ETC.

Dance to an easy 2/4 (3/4 or 6/8), a change in time signature lends different
qualities to the movement. Commence in first position.

BACK TO THE BARRE, arms outstretched sideways, fingertips lightly resting on
the barre. (Bars of music only noted below.)

Bars

1. *Battement tendu* side closing third or fifth position devant in *demi-plié*.
2. Repeat *battement tendu* side closing third or fifth position *derrière demi-plié* and
   using same foot.

Figures 102–104. Glissade dessus—first attempt, where toes
glide along the floor.

Figure 102. Demi-plié.

Figure 103. Pointe tendue.

Figure 104. Transfer weight and close fifth.

3. Stretch same foot *pointe tendue* side as far as possible whilst holding *fondu;* transfer weight through both feet to fall into *pointe tendue en fondu* on other leg without allowing either foot to move and keeping rest of body absolutely still.

4. Transfer weight back to original supporting leg with *pointe tendue en fondu.* Close first position, straightening both legs.

Repeat with other foot.

This exercise can also be practised forwards and backwards. Finally repeat in centre and on fourth bar, close the original supporting foot to the working foot, thus completing a *glissade* (figures 102–107 and note use of head, see p. 46).

Figures 105–107. Glissade dessus—second attempt. The black mark notes the distance travelled. N.B. The photographer has not moved.

Figure 105. Demi-plié in fifth.

Figure 106. Pointe tendue.

Figure 107. Transfer weight before close fifth.

Figures 108–110. Battements glissés and *jetés* must be firmly controlled.

Figure 108. On flat foot—front girl: at 18°; back girl: at 45°.

Figure 109. On *fondu*—front girl: at 18°; back girl: at 45°.

Figure 110. On *demi-pointe*—front girl: at 18°; back girl: at 45°.

Battements glissés en croix are an introduction to that controlled glided stretch and lift of the fully pointed working foot from the floor to an angle of 18°–30°, essential in much *terre à terre* work done at speed (figures 108–110). This is followed by a swift, but equally controlled closing which gives the child the first understanding of the rudiments of allegro. Such *glissés* must first be practised so that the working leg accents the movement equally outwards and inwards with strong pressure along the floor.

Any *glissé* movement below an angle of 30° comes ONLY from the foot and ankle. It is the push along the floor and ultimate stretching of that foot and ankle which gives the necessary impetus to lift the working leg from the floor. There is NO other movement in the leg and absolutely none from the hip.

As these movements are also vital preparatory movements for such steps as *assemblé* either *en place* or *porté* (travelled), they should often be practised commencing and finishing in a *demi-plié*, or opening on a *fondu* and more carefully timed.

(a) For *assemblé en place* the child should realise that the weight remains firmly fixed over the supporting leg as the working foot is pressed outwards and immediately back so that both feet are joined in position before the *demi-plié* begins (see Exercise 4).

(b) For *assemblé porté* however, the height of the raised leg will ultimately indicate the point at which the dancer will land from the jump, because he or she must follow the line of the toe downwards. As the foot leaves the floor to the required angle, the weight of the body is carried upwards and over as both feet join in the air to come down in the next position. For this exercise the leg must never be flung upwards. It must be absolutely controlled through the outwards *glissé* movement to the lift and momentarily held at its height before closing. Thus in practising it is useful to give time for a pause at the height of the *glissé*.

For example, Exercise 12 indicates the length of the step to be taken, but when danced with a *glissé* it indicates the length of the jump to be made when the child leaves the barre. Such exercises demonstrate clearly the wisdom of following the toe downwards and, if necessary, onwards for a proper transfer of weight from one foot to the other. This is in contrast to the transfer where the whole foot is glided along the floor in a *chassé* and the weight is simultaneously transferred to rest half-way between and over both feet (see Exercise 3).

Battements glissés strongly controlled at an angle of 18° or 30° are most valuable to introduce the delicate movement for *pointe work* called *piqué*, where the fully pointed foot lightly taps the floor and is quickly lifted again; or the dancer swiftly steps and carries her weight straight over on to the full *pointe* (*posé*). An amalgamation of *battements glissés* and *piqués* carefully timed lends speed and lightness to footwork. The following will help:

EXERCISE 13. *BATTEMENTS GLISSÉS* AND *PIQUÉS* TO LEND SPEED AND LIGHTNESS

Dance to eight bars of light 2/4. Commence third or fifth position and practise firstly to side with arm in second. Later perform *en croix* using the simplest form of *ports de bras*.

Bars

1. One *battement glissé* accenting equally outwards and inwards; open leg again on last half beat.
2. Two *battements glissés* accenting inwards and closing on beat.
3. One *battement glissé* outwards, *piqué* on second beat, i.e. drop and raise toe from floor.
4. Repeat *piqué* and close in third or fifth position, open on last half beat.
5–6. Three *battements glissés* accenting inwards movement. Close last on *demi-plié* and hold.
7. Stretch supporting knee with *glissé* outwards, *piqué*.
8. Two quick *battements piqués* and close in position.

IV. *Ronds de Jambe à Terre en dehors and en dedans*

Ronds de jambe help to cultivate the turn-out and teach the horizontal circling line required for all steps with a rounded form. They should be practised until the movement appears to originate from the hip of the turned-out leg, which is kept absolutely stretched throughout the *rond*, the toes, ankle and heel playing an independent part as the working foot passes through first position from back to front and vice-versa. When teaching *ronds de jambe à terre* it is best to prepare from first position as this helps to prevent the over-crossing of the working leg as it is stretched outwards. It is worth noting that whether the working foot moves from first or fifth position to *pointe tendue devant* or *derrière* it should reach exactly the same spot because from first position the weight will be slightly transferred over the supporting leg, therefore the working toe moves very slightly inwards to compensate for the slight transfer. But from fifth position it merely stretches directly forwards or backwards because no transfer is required (figures 111–114). Thus in neither case do the hips and shoulders lose their correct relationship to the centre line of balance and the buttock muscles should never jut out and fall back again with some rock of the pelvis (see p. 84).

During all forms of *ronds de jambe a terre* the working leg should be equidistant from the supporting leg during the *rond*. This can only happen if the weight is held firmly with spine erect (i.e. "tail" over heel). The heel of the working foot must be equally pushed forwards so that it passes exactly through first position on its way from front to back and vice-versa. Therefore emphasis should be made on maintaining the absolutely straight line from the hip to the middle toes of the working leg, so that when the foot reaches first position, it is properly bent at a right angle to its ankle and is at right angles to the front and back of the body. This means that all the muscles connecting foot to ankle, knee and hip will work equally to hold the leg in its correct alignment and NOT allow only the inside muscles of the leg to work with the resultant sickled foot.

92

Figures 111–114. Ronds de jambe en dehors in low and open
retiré to increase turn-out.

Figure 111. Attitude devant.

Figure 112. Open *retiré.*

Figure 113. Attitude derrière.

Figure 114. Open in low *arabesque* rising to *demi-pointe.*

Ronds de jambe à terre are first practised slowly, pausing at each point in the semi-circle and the closed position with a straight or bent supporting leg. This indicates the space both small and large which can be covered without displacing the central line of balance. Both arm and head should be used from the beginning (see p. 45) and as soon as possible a continuous circling should be encouraged. This circle can begin at any point, thus ensuring the circular shape is never lost. A series commencing from *pointe tendue* side is very valuable because a child often shortens the leg in the hip when moving to the side. Moreover this helps to regulate the timing of the circling for such movements as *pas de basque*.

Ronds de jambe à terre also points to another difference between work for boys and girls. Unlike the girl the boy is not encouraged to incline his head during the first attempts at slow *ronds de jambe* or *assemblés soutenus*. He directs his eyes forwards with the stretch to *pointe tendue devant*, turns his head to the side as the working leg reaches the side and only sometimes very slightly inclines his head over the supporting side as *pointe tendue derrière* is reached. He repeats the same head movements when moving *en dedans*.

Another important function of *ronds de jambe à terre* is to give greater co-ordination and thus some dancing quality to barre-work.

EXERCISE 14. *RONDS DE JAMBE A TERRE* WITH *PORTS DE BRAS* AND SMALL POSES

Dance to sixteen bars of stately waltz and keep up a continuous movement. Commence fifth position, with introductory bars breathe in and out, softly raising and lowering rounded arm at the side.

Bars

1. Breathe in, *fondu* stretching *pointe tendue devant*, raising arm to first position and inclining head over supporting leg.
2. Still breathing in (if possible) and holding *fondu*, circle to side opening arm to second position and turning head to side.
3. Holding breath and *fondu*, circle to *pointe tendue derrière*, leaving arm in second position but slightly lifting head.
4. Breathe out, passing leg through first *demi-plié*, dropping arm to *bras bas* lowering head a little forwards.
5. Breathe in, stretching spine well upwards and leg to *pointe tendue devant* on first beat continuing into one complete *rond en dehors* gradually lifting arm and raising head so that by first beat of bar –
6. The arm is in first position and the working leg is commencing a second *rond*. Follow the movement of the arm upwards with the eyes, so that with an intake of breath and by the first beat of bar –
7. The arm is in fifth position and the leg is commencing a third *rond*. Hold the arm momentarily in fifth position, eyes glancing inside palm and then gradually open arm sideways so that by first beat of bar:—
8. Arm has reached second position and is falling into *bras bas* as leg continues into fourth *rond*.

9–12. Repeat bars 5–8 so that by first beat of bar –

13. Working foot pauses *pointe tendue devant*, arm lowered to *bras bas*.

14. Gradually rising to *demi-pointe* (supporting leg) pass working leg through first position, raising arm to well rounded first, slightly inclining head over supporting side.

15–16. Continue raising leg into low *arabesque* also stretch arm to *arabesque* line, lift, slightly turn and glance towards raised leg. Remove hand from barre and balance *à deux bras*. Repeat in reverse, reversing arm so that on the first beat of bar 5, the arm is raised from second to fifth position, falls to first in bar 6, to *bras bas* in bar 7 and is raised again to second in bar 8. This movement is repeated in bars 9–12 and then moves from first to second position or *arabesque* before the supporting hand leaves the barre to be held *à deux bras* or in an open fourth position.

This is an extremely good exercise for correct breathing, and to remind children that the "gap" between the lower ribs and thighs must always be maintained.

The practice of small and very exact quarter *ronds* as noted in Exercise 8 but without the *demi-pliés* or *fondus* will help those inclined to work slowly or inaccurately as they neaten the footwork.

Finally there are special forms of *ronds de jambe* to improve turn-out.

EXERCISE 15. *RONDS DE JAMBE À TERRE* TO IMPROVE TURN-OUT AND AS A PREPARATION FOR *GRANDS RONDS DE JAMBE EN L'AIR*

Dance to a slow flowing waltz with a continuous movement throughout. Commence *pointe tendue derrière*, hold arm in second position.

Bars

1. Swing leg through first position and with a strong action from the heel along the floor push upwards to a low *attitude devant*, upper part of leg from hip to knee must be as turned-out as possible, hips level and facing same plane as shoulders.

2. Holding leg at this open angle, circle upper half of the leg to the side, ensuring that the toe falls in an absolutely straight line under the knee.

3. Continue circling the upper half of the leg to the back, as far as possible maintaining the same angle and height by "tilting" slightly forwards from the hip-joint, but raising the lower half from knee to toe into a low *attitude*, remembering that for *attitude* it is only necessary to bend the lower half of the leg inwards from the knee so that the upper half comes behind the torso.

4. Stretch the raised leg outwards and downwards into a low *arabesque* before finishing *pointe tendue derrière*, and repeat from the beginning (figures 111–114).

This exercise should be repeated four times in all *en dehors*, and then *en dedans*. In the latter it commences *pointe tendue devant*, the working leg being swung through first position with a strong action along the floor before being lifted into a low *attitude* as above and with the same "tilt" of the pelvis. The tilted pelvis is then straightened as the leg reaches the side.

If this exercise is to be effective the upper half of the leg does most of the work. The angle must be held firmly until the *attitudes* are reached and only then does the knee straighten. Each dancer will find the exact point to stretch upwards with an intake of breath in order to maintain the "gap" and "tilt" (*en dehors*) or straighten (*en dedans*). This is also the exact moment when the pelvis will have to "tilt" or straighten in *grands ronds de jambe*.

V. *Grands Battements*

The main purpose of *grands battements* is to loosen and strengthen the limbs as well as eventually establish the height at which the leg should be held. In the initial stages they should be practised as *battements glissés*, but at that moment when the fully stretched leg is pulled upwards by the impetus of the foot along the floor, this impetus must be reinforced by the action of the muscles in the upper leg and pelvis playing a proper part in "throwing" the leg still higher. Once again the spine must be erect, hips and shoulders facing the same plane. There is a slight "tilt" of the pelvis forwards when moving to the back. But no matter in which direction the *battement* is directed, the buttock muscles must be drawn together, BUT NEVER TENSED, those inside and in front of the leg must be stretched outwards from the hip-joint, and those of the stomach and rib-cage must be lifted upwards to ensure that the leg moves freely within the "gap". The weight must always be held over the supporting leg, which should never move out of the perpendicular. Such a movement is extremely difficult for those with sway-back legs. But with perseverance and a strictly controlled "THROW" of the leg, all but those with most exaggerated forms of sway-back can manage, if they are prepared to hold their weight well forwards over the supporting leg with the knee NOT pulled back, BUT UP. When they move to the back they must remember to "tilt" and not "rock" the pelvis (see p. 19).

As soon as the elementary *grands battements* are mastered, exercises should be given to loosen the legs still further and increase the amount of control needed to maintain the height of the leg. The following is a guide to what is required and also introduces that strong movement needed later to impel the dancer upwards into such steps as *grands fouettés*, *grands jetés* etc.

EXERCISE 16. *GRANDS BATTEMENTS EN CROIX* TO LOOSEN AND INCREASE THE CONTROL OF THE LEG IN ALL POSES AND GRAND ELEVATION

Dance to two bars of 4/4, i.e. eight bars in all when repeated *en croix*. Commence in first, third or fifth position and hold arm in second or fifth position for front and side and lower to *arabesque* for back.

Bars
1. (i–ii) *Grand battement devant* as high as possible and close. (iii–iv) Repeat above *battement*.
2. (i) Breathe in throwing leg upwards. (ii–iii) Hold at highest point possible without in any way displacing the supporting leg or the carriage of the body.

(iv) Close.

Repeat to side and then to back and side again.

This exercise should also be danced to a slow easy waltz. This timing helps to establish the need to hold the pose, i.e.

First bar: (i) Raise leg. (ii) Hold. (iii) Close.

Second bar: Repeat first bar.

Third and Fourth bars. *Battement* on first beat and do not close until last beat of fourth bar.

As well as increasing the height and control over the working leg, *grands battements* amalgamated with rises or *relevés* to *demi-pointe* are most strengthening (see p. 39).

EXERCISE 17. *GRANDS BATTEMENTS EN CROIX* TO GIVE GREATER STRENGTH, CONTROL AND BREADTH TO ALL POSES

Dance to four bars of Grand March 2/4, or eight bars of well accented waltz. Commence fifth position *bras bas*. Boys should use rise, and girls *relevé*. (N.B. sixteen bars of 2/4 are needed if danced *en croix*.)

Bars

1. (i) *Relevé* (or rise) raising arm to first position; (ii) *Grand battement devant* opening arm to second position.

2. (i) Close feet together on *demi-pointe* holding arm in second position and lift hand momentarily from the barre. (ii) Lower heels and push into small *demi-plié*. Straighten knees.

3–4. Two *grands battements devant*, dropping arms *bras bas* on last beat. Repeat moving to side and then back. Always move arm to second position as this stabilises the return to *demi-pointe*.

Later the whole can be repeated on *demi-pointe*, dropping into *demi-plié* at the end of each four bar sequence.

Grands battements can also be used instead of *battements tendus* in Exercise 8, where a quick circling of the leg at 45° or 90° helps to strengthen and stabilise the movement for quick *grands ronds de jambe*. Similarly if they are used at 45° or 90° instead of *battements glissés* and *piqués* as in Exercise 13, the child soon understands the need to keep the working leg moving independently in its socket if he or she is going to keep all types of allegro work light and accurate.

Similarly, *grands battements* can eventually be used instead of *battements tendus* in Exercise 7 to help children to maintain the "gap" between hips and rib-cage at all times thus giving the leg more freedom to move in any direction. Sometimes the working leg should be allowed to fall on to a straight leg when moving to the open position, and sometimes into a *demi-plié*. In both cases the weight must be transferred equally between the two feet and as soon as the return lift is made, the weight must be replaced over the supporting leg. In moving to the *demi-plié* it is essential that the working toe and heel reach the floor before the knees begin to relax and on returning to the closed position, the toe must be fully stretched and the weight returned with the supporting knee straight before the leg is lifted from the floor.

A variation of the above is extremely valuable for boys. Correctly performed it can make them understand the "force" necessary to push the weight of the body into the air by the proper use of the foot, floor and the strength of the back muscles.

EXERCISE 18. *GRAND BATTEMENTS EN CROIX* INTO A LUNGE

Dance to a steady strong 2/4 (eight bars when danced *en croix*). Commence third or fifth position, arms held in second. Later arm in fifth.

Bars

1. (i) *Grand battement devant* and as soon as *pointe tendue* is reached on descent (ii) drop heel and transfer weight over to working leg *en fondu* by relaxing achilles tendon, knee and hip-joint. The supporting leg must be kept straight, foot flat to floor. A straight line should be seen from the head to the instep of the supporting leg (figure 44).
2. (i) With a strong push from the floor, lift working leg and transfer weight back to supporting leg without bending knee or losing control over erect spine, "tail" pulled down and pelvis still. (ii) Close fifth position. Repeat to side and back.

The latter is very difficult for all but those with very straight legs. But it can help to strengthen and correct various defects because of the control exercised by all the muscles from shoulders to toes (figure 46 which shows boy's first attempt at this).

Grands battements développés are practised to teach how to control the full but quick extension of the leg in the air, and should not be attempted until the child has gained some understanding of slow *développés* (see p. 108). This is also the case with *Battements retirés*.

VI. *Petits Battements and Battements Frappés* (figures 115–117)

The practice of these types of *battements* leads to a proper performance of beaten steps in which the action of the legs from the knees through ankle, instep and toes has to be strong yet precise and light. Unlike *battements tendus* where the stretch of the whole leg is important and *battements glissés* where the vital impetus comes from the ankle and foot, in both *petits battements* and *battements frappés*, the impetus comes only from the knee downwards whilst the rest of the leg remains absolutely still.

The difference in action to be made between *petits battements* and *battements frappés* depends firstly on a correct preparation. The child must understand that during *petits battements*, which are an introduction to the various *entrechats*, the tips of the toes lightly trace a line outwards and inwards on the floor, because the impetus for such jumps comes from the *demi-plié* and the two feet will beat equally when the body rises into the air.

But in *battements frappés* introducing beaten *assemblés*, the tips of the toes lead the ball of the foot (metatarsal arch), which pushes into and outwards from the floor in a straight line, because the impetus for the jump comes from the working foot as the supporting leg bends, straightens and jumps from a *fondu*.

Figure 115. Front. Girl prepares for *petits battements*; centre girl prepares for *battements frappés*; last girl in *petit retiré.*

Figure 116. The same on *demi-pointe*, the last girl in *fondu* ready to stretch for *battement fondu à terre* from 18° to 45°.

Figure 117. Battement fondu at 45° as used in R.A.D. Note difference between *retiré* for work *à terre* and that for work at 45°.

(a) *Petits Battements*

The simplest way for a child to find the correct position for *petits battements* is to stretch the working foot *pointe tendue* sideways; bend the foot upwards at right angles with toes and instep stretched; bend the knee, bringing the foot inwards until the middle of the instep (below the foot) rests just above the ankle bone of the turned-out supporting leg; then stretch instep and toes downwards until the tips of the toes rest on the floor (figure 115). They must not be bent in any way. Even if the foot is large, there must be no contraction of the instep, curling of the toes, nor sickling of the foot outwards to wrap round the ankle. From this position the lower half of the leg moves outwards and inwards from the knee only and from the front to the back of the supporting leg or vice-versa. The foot must be seen to rest momentarily as far across the back as across the front of the supporting leg. The tips of the toes thus trace an acute angle at the side of the supporting leg without any effort being made in any muscles above the knee. These only come into play as the first beaten *changements* or *entrechats* are practised, when both fully stretched legs have to open and close swiftly once or twice as the body ascends from and descends into a *demi-plié*. It is also useful to note that when *petits battements* are practised with the supporting foot on *demi-pointe*, the working foot must be stretched further downwards. This important detail should be stressed before attempting any beaten movement such as *petits battements battus devant* or *derrière* used as an introduction to *cabrioles* and certain steps in *pointe-work*.

Petits Battements should be first practised moving equally backwards and forwards so that the action is smooth and the knee, although held firmly outwards, is never tense. Once an evenly timed and equalised movement is achieved, the timing, accent and detail of the beaten step to follow should be attempted.

Exercise 19. *PETITS BATTEMENTS* AS AN INTRODUCTION TO *CHANGEMENTS BATTUS* OR *ENTRECHATS QUATRE*

Dance to four bars of steady 2/4. Commence *sur le cou de pied devant*, prepared as stated above.

Bars

1. Move foot outwards and close behind; then return to front, slightly marking each beat.
2. Repeat above two movements to back and front.
3. Repeat above two movements twice, but as they are quicker, there should be a slight emphasis on the return *sur le cou de pied devant*, as there would be if two *entrechats quatre* had been performed.
4. Open leg slightly sideways, return and beat *sur le cou de devant*, re-open and draw foot backwards *sur le cou de pied derrière*, as if a *changement battu* had been performed.

   Repeat reversing whole so that the slightly accented movement occurs behind and not in front of the supporting leg.

There can be many variations of this type of *petits battements*. The following is a valuable exercise to help children understand how the beat should be felt throughout the legs from hips to toes.

EXERCISE 20. *PETITS BATTEMENTS* TO ENCOURAGE FULLY STRETCHED LEGS IN *ENTRECHATS*, ETC.

Dance to four bars of steady 2/4, facing with both hands on barre. Commence fifth position right foot front.

Bars

1. *Relevé* (girls), rise (boys), bend working foot up at right angles to leg, foot must be fully stretched and inside leg muscles pulled well downwards. Inside of legs touch each other.
2. Holding leg thus stretched with foot at an angle, move it well outwards and then behind supporting leg move it outwards and return to front of supporting leg (figure 118).
3. Repeat bar 2.
4. Replace ball of working foot on floor so that both feet are now on *demi-pointe*, drop heels and relax into *demi-plié*.

   Repeat, using left foot so that movement commences from the back. Then repeat with left foot so that both are used equally. The essential detail is to keep the working leg fully turned-out and stretched so that the child can feel the insides of both legs meet each time they are closed together, and there is a sufficiently wide space between the legs so that they can be seen well apart at each opening.

(b) *Battements Frappés*

Battements frappés should also be prepared from a *pointe tendue* to the side, but when the foot is drawn back to rest across the supporting ankle as above, the toes should not be lowered so far because the tips of the toes have to lead the ball of the foot (i.e. metatarsal arch) which pushes slightly into and out of the floor at an angle until the leg is fully stretched because the ball of the foot must give sufficient impetus to carry the body towards the spot under which the dancer will land when a darting jump is performed (figure 115).

However in addition to introducing a child to the strong impetus required to propel the body along and into the air for *assemblés* where the accent is outwards, *battements frappés* are also a valuable introduction to *entrechats trois, cinq etc.*, *flic-flac* and other beaten steps where the accent is inwards. Therefore, because these movements are so valuable as preparations they should be practised to many different timings with different accenting and amalgamated with other movements.

They must first be practised to the side only, as this gives greater strength to every movement and should be timed so that the strongest accent is outwards, the leg being thrust outwards from *sur le cou de pied devant* until it is fully stretched from the knee through ankle to toe, which pauses 2–3 inches from the floor, i.e. at exactly the same height reached by the toe in *battements glissés*. It is then brought back *sur le cou de pied derrière*, the knee and foot at ankle being bent simultaneously before they reach the supporting leg.

Once the sideways movement has been mastered, *battements frappés* should be practised *en croix*. With each outwards thrust the leg must be kept fully turned-out, the knee and foot being returned *sur le cou de pied* at exactly the same angle at which the *battement* began, i.e. fully turned-out. This is particularly important when returning from *frappé derrière*, where there must be exactly the same careful stretch upwards of the body and holding of weight over the supporting leg as in *battements tendus derrière* (see p. 84). Later they should be practised *en croix* using a *petit battement* before each *frappé* as an introduction to *assemblés battus*, and also with a *fondu* or rise on the supporting leg with the outwards movement so that the pose can be held *fondu à terre* or *relevé en l'air*, the actual position being determined by the action of the supporting leg, because the height of the working leg should not vary if the movement is done correctly from the knee only.

Battements Frappés as Preparation for Flic-flac

It is valuable to practise a form of *battement frappé* in which the working foot does not move outwards with friction on the floor to give impetus (i.e. a slightly curving-under movement), but springs outwards with a slightly curving-over movement so that the tips of the toes alone reach the floor, as they would when stepping into a *posé*. The foot should commence *sur le cou de pied* with the toes stretched downwards. From thence it is slightly and swiftly drawn up the supporting leg before being thrust outwards to *pointe tendue*. After this the foot is "sucked" back *sur le cou de pied devant* or *derrière* by gently pressing and pushing the ball and then the heel along the floor before being brought upwards over the ankle as in a preparation for *flic-flac*. This is a very strengthening movement for the ankle and toes.

VII. *Battements Fondus and Ballottés*

(a) *Battements fondus* are invaluable for teaching children how to co-ordinate movements where both legs have to stretch simultaneously in different directions. It teaches them more than any other exercise how to maintain balance over the supporting leg. As in *battements frappés* the main action appears to come from the knee of the working leg downwards, but it is the relaxation into and push out of the floor exercised by all the muscles of the supporting leg, which ultimately gives the child strength to sustain the powerful stretch upwards and outwards to front, side or back of the working leg. The action is identical to that of a *demi-plié*.

The preparation for *battements fondus* should be from *pointe tendue* to side and on the first beat of the music, the working foot should be drawn slowly back to *sur le cou de pied devant* simultaneously with a bend of the supporting knee. This usually means that the working foot is bent upwards at a greater angle because the supporting leg is *fondu* and sustains the whole weight of the body. (*N.B.* the "tail" should be seen to be directly over the heel of the supporting foot). From

Figure 118. Special exercise for *entrechats.*

(*a*) Rise to *demi-pointe.*

(*b*) Bend foot at ankle.

(*c*) Open leg straight to side.

(*d*) Close foot behind.

(*e*) Press raised foot back to *demi-pointe.*

this position, the supporting leg straightens and pushes the body upwards as the working knee and ankle gradually stretch until the toe rests *pointe tendue* side. Once the slow closing and opening of the working leg from the knee downwards is mastered together with the slow relaxation and push of the supporting leg, *battements fondus* should be practised *en croix*. As in *battements frappés* there must be that same careful return of the turned-out working knee and foot to the correct *sur le cou de pied* position at the end of each stretching movement.

Later *battements fondus* at 45° must be practised because a working leg held at this height, or over, plays a large part in adagio. For this movement the position *sur le cou de pied* is at the same height as before. As the movement of the working leg outwards comes from the knee only, the preparatory movement should be made from a *battement jeté* to the side (i.e. raise the fully stretched leg to an angle of 45°). From here the lower half of the leg alone bends inwards until the toes of the fully stretched foot rest on the centre of the supporting leg, either in front or behind, in most cases the tips of the toes are roughly on a level with the ankle bone. From this position the leg is stretched outwards as it was when stretching *à terre*. This requires greater control and strength if the height of the knee is to be maintained. The movement must be equally sustained outwards and inwards as the supporting leg is pressed downwards by the weight of the body and then reacts to push the body and working leg upwards to its original starting point.

This change from a passive to an active function becomes even more difficult when the dancer rises to *demi-pointe* on the supporting leg. The action of pushing upwards must be carefully analysed, although it must be performed very smoothly and continuously. The supporting knee must be felt to straighten before the heel begins to push upwards to *demi-pointe* and the working leg stretched to its fullest simultaneously with the supporting leg completing its action.

It must be remembered when performing *battements fondus derrière*, as in every other type of movement backwards, that there must be a careful "tilt" of the pelvis as the weight of the body is carried firmly but slightly forwards whenever the leg is raised beyond 18°. This "tilt" must be accompanied by the strong stretch upwards of the spine and lift of the head.

A simple *ports de bras* using the counter-pull of forces and a strict enforcement of the law of opposition always helps children to gain confidence when *battements fondus* are first practised in the centre (see p. 52).

(b) *Ballottés*. Practising *ballottés* at the barre is another valuable exercise for co-ordinating the movement of the legs when they have to stretch and/or relax simultaneously, particularly when the movement ultimately develops into a step of *grand elevation*. *Ballottés* require absolute control and a perfect transfer of weight at the height of the jump, so that the rocking to and fro of the body and legs does resemble the rocking of a boat, which gives the step its name. However the movement should first be practised slowly at the barre to enable the dancer to "feel" the centering of balance as the weight is transferred through the feet in *demi-pointe* in fifth position.

When dancing in the centre the movement only rocks forwards and backwards, but at the barre it should first be practised *en croix* before attempts are made to transfer the weight from one leg to the other because such exercises are useful in strengthening the spine as well as the legs.

The preparation for any *ballotté* exercise should be from *pointe tendue* side, the supporting leg *fondu*. The working foot is drawn or "sucked" into fifth *devant* simultaneously with a stretch upwards of the supporting leg, both feet arriving together on *demi-pointe*. It is essential to perform this movement accurately and without pause so that both knees are straight and heels together in fifth position before both feet stretch upwards together to *demi-pointe*. From this position the supporting leg relaxes into *fondu*, the movement passing through *petit retiré* before stretching forwards. From thence the working leg is again drawn into fifth position, so that both legs arrive together on *demi-pointe*. The exercise continues *en croix*, the working leg moving to the side, closing fifth *derrière* on *demi-pointe*, then backwards and lastly to the side.

It is most important to note that every time the feet join and rise together in fifth *demi-pointe*, the weight is centred over both feet and, as the working leg is raised to *petit retiré*, is firmly transferred to the supporting leg as this relaxes into *fondu*. Another important point is to allow the body a little license so that when the working leg unfolds forwards the body inclines slightly backwards, with a stretch of the cervical spine, and very slightly towards the barre from the waist upwards as the working leg moves to the side, and is "tilted" forwards from the pelvis with the same stretching of the spine required in any *arabesque* when the leg moves backwards. If the spine is allowed to play this part at the barre, it is so much easier to make the necessary adjustments to the transfer of weight when *ballottés* are practised *à terre* with a *développé* in 90° in adagios, or are used with a spring in *petit* or *grand elevation* in allegro. Without some body movement this step has no style or quality (see also p. 118).

VIII. *Petits Ronds de Jambe en l'air*

Petits ronds de jambe en l'air lend a light delicate air to Classical Dance, particularly to solos for ballerinas. It is also another movement which takes place from the knee downwards, the lower half of the working leg describing a small circle *en dehors* or *en dedans* whilst apparently hanging loose in the air. These *ronds* should be practised with great care as a jerk or twist can easily tear or misplace the delicate cartilage within the knee.

In the first stages of practise the well turned-out working leg should be raised sideways to an angle of 45° and followed by an attempt to describe a small semi-circle in the air in front of the supporting leg. The knee must be relaxed, and there must be no tension in the hip, ankle, or foot which is fully pointed. Perhaps the easiest way for a child to understand the delicacy of the movement, which takes place in front of and not behind the supporting leg is as follows:

EXERCISE 21. PREPARATORY EXERCISE FOR *PETITS RONDS DE JAMBE EN L'AIR*

Dance to slow 2/4, later 3/4. Commence third or fifth *devant*. Arm held in second position throughout. Practise at 45° only.

A. *En dehors*

1. (i) Slow *battement glissé* side to 45°. (ii) Keeping upper half of leg firm and held sideways, relax lower half into *retiré*.

2. (i) Still keeping upper half of leg firm and still, circle lower half as if moving into *attitude devant*. Keep inside of leg upmost in an attempt to retain turn-out; open lower half to side without dropping knee. (ii) Close fifth *derrière*.

B. *En dedans*

1. (i) Slow *battement glissé* as above. (ii) Keeping upper half of leg still, circle lower half as if moving into *attitude devant*, again keeping inside of leg upmost to retain turn-out.

2. (i) Circle lower half into *retiré*, open to side. (ii) Close fifth *devant*.

This exercise only introduces children to the effort required to circle the lower half of the leg within a confined area without strain. If they are to understand the impetus required to perform such a movement when dancing, and using a *relevé* or jump on the supporting leg, the following can help. It commences with a *chassé* forwards or backwards so that the working foot is put under some pressure before being lifted into the *rond*. This gives greater strength, accuracy and speed to the tiny circling movement.

EXERCISE 22. *CHASSÉ* INTO *PETITS RONDS DE JAMBE EN L'AIR*

Dance to four bars mazurka. Commence fifth position and use simple *ports de bras*.

Bars

1. (i) *Chassé* forwards into *demi-plié* fourth opposite fifth position raising arm to first. (ii) Straighten supporting knee and simultaneously raise fully stretched working leg front. (iii) Carry it to side at 45°, opening arm to second position.

2. (i–ii) One *petit rond de jambe en l'air en dehors* (later use two, one to each beat. (iii) Close fifth *derrière*.
   Repeat *en dedans* moving first into *chassé* backwards before lifting and circling leg from back to side.
   Children should practise *petits ronds* slowly in a series and directed in one way only, before attempting to repeat the movement alternately *en dehors* and *en dedans*. Once they are mastered in a series, it is comparatively simple to increase the number of *ronds* before the leg descends into fifth position.

IX. *Raising the Straight Leg to Front, Side and Back*

It is important to teach children, particularly boys, to raise their working leg to 45° and later 90° before they practise *développés* as this gives them a better understanding of how to pull upon all the muscles of buttocks, thighs, abdomen and waist to achieve height without displacing the hip line and twisting the rest of the body out of alignment. If *grands battements* have been practised properly they will have a good idea of what has to be done (Exercise 17, p. 97). But the raising of the leg (*relevé* in the Russian School) should be slower and absolutely continuous until the leg reaches the required height.

A correct use of the *ports de bras* plays a useful part as the movement of the arm should coincide with that of the leg and help the child to breathe correctly whilst holding the body still. The preparatory *ports de bras* (see p. 79) is used no matter in which direction the leg is raised. The arm reaches first position when the leg is half-way towards the required height and completes its move to second position a fraction of a second AFTER the leg has reached its fullest height. It is most valuable to use this *ports de bras* when stretching the leg into *arabesque* as it helps to keep the shoulders square and level and prevents the arm reaching its fullest stretch before the leg. Only when proper co-ordination has been attained should the arm be allowed to straighten into an *arabesque* line AFTER the final stretch of the leg.

Later it is useful to raise the arm to fifth position when raising the leg to front and side as this gives a greater feeling of strength and stretch to the body.

Développés to Front, Side and Back

Practised individually these give great strength to all movements of the legs, as the effort of slowly unfolding the working leg at any angle from 45° to 90° or even higher, requires the use of all the important muscles of the body. Although it is comparatively easy for a child to lift the leg into the preliminary *retiré* before the stretch into a *développé*, it is not easy to maintain the height at which the leg must unfold. This is indicated by the height of the bent knee. Therefore the child should first practise lifting the working leg to the required height in a series of *retirés* in order to realise the control needed when the leg has to be unfolded.

A Proper Retiré

This movement ideally commences from fifth position as it ensures the weight is correctly centred before the movement begins. It can also be practised from first or third position, which is valuable at early stages when practising for jumps such as *temps levés*.

From fifth position the working foot should be swiftly pointed when the knee bends to lift it from the floor, so that the tips of the toes all but touch the centre of the fully turned-out supporting leg just at the ankle bone. From thence it is brought straight and slightly diagonally upwards until the tips of the toes rest at the side of the supporting leg, the working knee pausing at the required height for the movement to follow.

Because the *retiré* must be swift and economical the track is all important, particularly when it is remembered that the *retiré* at 45° is the ideal height at which to hold the working foot during first attempts at *pirouettes*. A *retiré* at 90° however, results in a better *développé*, therefore when first practised on their own in a series passing from front to back and vice-versa, i.e. *retirés passés*, the movement must be to the exact height and smooth and continuous. There must be no hint of syncopation, no strange *petit battement* from front to back when the *retiré* reaches its height. Once this is mastered, it should be pointed out that a *retiré* for a *pirouette* requires a hold at the height of the movement. But for a *relevé passé* and for *développé* the movement should be equally timed upwards and downwards, particularly for the former, when a girl will ultimately be expected to perform a series of *relevés retirés passés sur les pointes*. It is quite useful to use a waltz when practising *retirés* as a preparation for *pirouettes*, but a 2/4 or 4/4 rhythm when practising *retirés passés*.

Once children can control and hold a *retiré* they must realise that as soon as the upper half of the well turned-out working leg reaches any angle between 45° and 90° (or even higher) at the side of the supporting leg, the knee remains at that height during the stretch into *développé*. From this position the lower half of the leg, directed by the toe of a well pointed foot, slowly unfolds upwards so that:

(a) If the leg moves front, the upper half only moves forwards as the lower half unfolds, the working hip remains still and the muscles on the inside and under the upper half play their proper part to maintain height and control the stretch of the whole leg.

(b) If the leg moves sideways, the upper half remains absolutely still and the lower half ONLY moves upwards until the centre of the front of the leg faces the ceiling, or is parallel to ceiling and floor if the leg is stretched outwards at an angle of 90°. It is during this *développé* that there is a tendency to sickle the foot outwards, which immediately throws the supporting hip out of alignment.

(c) If the leg moves backwards, the upper half of the leg also moves backwards (as in Exercise 15, p. 95) with a slight movement of the lower leg upwards to pass through *attitude* as the pelvis "tilts" slightly forwards before the leg is finally stretched into *arabesque*.

During the first exercises for *développés* the simple *ports de bras* should be used, i.e. the arm rises from *bras bas* to first position with the *retiré* and opens to second position just after the leg has stretched to its fullest. Later the arm can be used as it was when raising the leg straight upwards from the closed position.

Later an exercise should be developed to give an even greater sense of control, breadth and balance to an adagio as in the following exercise, which incorporates correct breathing with an altogether fuller stretch and slight movement of the arm and body.

This exercise is developed through three stages. The first merely requires the child to perform *développés en croix* with a simple *ports de bras*, breathing in and out with each *développé*.

The second stage requires the child to perform *développés en croix*, taking two breaths with each *développé*, so that there is an inhalation with the *retiré*, exalation as the leg unfolds; and another inhalation as the leg is held and the arm raised to fifth position; and an exhalation as the leg closes in fifth position. It should be danced to a steady 6/8 time.

The third stage requires the child to use three breaths with each *développé en croix* and is danced to a slow sarabande or 4/4. Commence fifth position. *Bras bas.*

Bars

1. Breath in, raising leg to *retiré* and arm to first position; breathe out and unfold leg front, opening arm to second position.
2. Breathe in, raising arm to fifth position and hold before breathing out.
3. Breathe in, stretching upwards and bending slightly backwards.
4. Recover, breathe out lowering arm and leg.
5–8. Repeat but *développé* side, using same breathing and bend sideways towards the barre.
9–12. Repeat to *arabesque*, but do not close on last beat of phrase.
13–16. Breathe in, lowering arm and body into *penché*, with the exhalation try and relax at waist-line without contracting at "gap", i.e. the spine actually moves into a straight line. Breathe in and return body and arm to *arabesque*, trying to stretch the leg even further upwards and backwards and the body more forwards and lifted from the waist. With the final breath, take hand off barre and hold *arabesque*. It is also useful to rise on *demi-pointe* before taking hand off barre (figures 119–123).

XI. *Demi- and Grands Ronds de Jambe, Rotation and Grands Fouettés*

The action of the body "bowing" forwards or straightening from the "tilt" of the pelvis over the supporting leg is the same in all the above movements. It occurs as the working leg circles in the air from side to back or back to side. But there must be a clear understanding of the difference between these three important movements of adagio and *grand elevation*.

In *grands ronds de jambe* the working leg and body do all the work. The supporting leg remains absolutely still either fully stretched and perpendicular to the floor, or in *fondu* with the "tail" held immediately over the supporting heel.

In *rotation* most of the effort is made by the supporting leg with the help of the body, which adjusts itself to two quarter turning movements whilst the working leg remains fully stretched and comparatively still.

In *grandes fouettés* both working and supporting legs play an equal part in making a half turn. The working leg gives the impetus for the supporting leg to become active and spring, rise or *relevé* just before the body adjusts itself to the turning movement as it does in *rotation*.

(a) *Grands Ronds de Jambe en l'air (also Demi-ronds)*

During the *en dehors* movement: after the initial *développé* or raising of the leg *devant* and circle to the side, the child must stretch the body upwards with an intake of breath and "tilt" the pelvis forwards as the leg circles from side to back. The "tilt" must be accomplished smoothly so that he or she feels the working leg is being stretched away from the hip-joint to complete the semi-circle because it is weightless. All the weight is retained over the supporting leg because space has been made between hip-joint and ribs in which to make adjustments to the turn-out at hip level. Thus, if the intake of breath and the resultant lift of the body from the waist as the pelvis "tilts" is done correctly, the height of the working leg can be maintained. Moreover both hips and shoulders should remain level and facing the same plane. If necessary a slight adjustment of the hand on the barre can help (see p. 34). It is also helpful to raise the working arm to fifth position when the leg reaches side, and lower it to *arabesque* with the final movement of the leg. This *ports de bras* helps to ensure that the weight is equally distributed over the supporting leg after the pelvis has "tilted" because the body and the working leg appear to be equally stretched away from the central perpendicular line of balance. This is particularly important when the final pose of *arabesque* has to be held.

During the *en dedans* movement, the child has to make the adjustment from a tilted pelvis to an erect position as the leg moves from back to side. The exact point for the upwards stretch often depends on the shape of the hips. Those with large hips and small waists need to begin their adjustment slightly sooner than those with narrow hips and average waists. It is at this point (roughly at 45° or midway between back and side) where an intake of breath helps to stretch the body erect and a pull on the muscles of buttocks and thighs of the working leg inwards and round helps to maintain the turn-out with hips level. As in *grands ronds en dehors*, the raising of the arm from *arabesque* to fifth position helps to stretch the spine upwards and prevents a collapse of the body into the hip-joint on the working side.

(b) *Rotation*

During *rotation* the supporting leg makes two quarter turning movements *en place* when performed slowly, whilst the working leg is apparently held raised and still at the same height. This turning movement is best understood when practised with a *fondu* and a rise or *relevé* on the supporting leg as the child turns from front to side, and side to back, and vice-versa.

However it is a mistake to believe that the working leg remains exactly over the same spot throughout the *rotation*. Such an idea only leads to over-crossing, because the hips and shoulders twice change their relationship to the legs. Nevertheless if the working leg is stretched away from the hip-joint and kept as still as possible, the slight adjustments necessary are hardly noticeable.

These slight adjustments in the relationship of the working leg to the hips and shoulders occur during the two quarter turns which must remain level as

Figures 119–123. Développés and breathing.

Figure 119. Retiré.

Figure 120. Développé devant.

Figure 121. First attempts at stretching spine up and a little back.

Figure 122. Développé to *arabesque.*

Figure 123. First attempts at *penché.*

they turn to their new front. The adjustments are best studied by trying *rotation à terre*.

Preliminary rotation exercise only

Commence fifth position *éffacé* and stretch *pointe tendue devant*, *fondu*, which, if done correctly, means that the working toe will slide slightly away from the supporting leg because the weight remains firmly fixed over its central point (i.e., "tail" over heel). This gives the child the idea of stretching outwards. Rise or *relevé* to *demi-pointe* making a quarter turn into *écarté devant* and lower heel, the working toe should move very slightly forwards if it is to remain in the same line as the hip and not over-cross; *fondu*, the working toe again slides slightly away from the supporting heel if the weight remains correctly centred; rise of *relevé* on to *demi-pointe* making another quarter turn into *arabesque à terre;* the working leg again moves very slightly as both hips and shoulders move round to come square and face the same plane as the weight is carried more forwards over the supporting leg.

Once the above is mastered the *rotation* must be practised with the working leg raised to an angle of 90° (figures 124–126).

EXERCISE 24. EXERCISE FOR ROTATION

Dance to four bars of sarabande or eight bars of slow waltz. Commence fifth *bras bas*.

Bars
1. (or two bars waltz). *Développé devant* opening arm through first to second position, breathing in and out.
2. Bend supporting leg (*fondu*) and hold working leg firmly outstretched so that it is seen to sink with the *fondu*.
3. Breathing in, rise (or *relevé*) on to *demi-pointe* making a quarter turn bringing the body round to face the barre, keeping the hips and shoulders level and the working arm in second position.
4. Breathe out and *fondu*, holding the working leg firmly outstretched so that it is seen to sink with the *fondu*.
5. Breathe in and rise (or *relevé*) on to *demi-pointe* lifting the body upwards from the waist and making the quarter turn to bring hips and shoulders to the new front simultaneously tilting the pelvis forwards as the working leg moves to *arabesque* and the supporting leg sinks to *fondu*. At the movement of the quarter turn, the supporting hand must leave the barre to be replaced by the other hand. But it must be remembered, because the pelvis "tilts" forwards for the *arabesque*, the new supporting hand should not touch the barre until the shoulders are square to the new front.

6–7–8. Hold and close on last beat.

En dedans: when rotating *en dedans*, the above action is reversed and, as in *grands ronds de jambe en dedans*, the working leg must be felt to be gradually drawn round and turned outwards by the pull of the muscles in buttocks and thighs.

Figure 124. Fondu and *développé devant.*

Figure 125. Breathe in, rise on *demi-pointe,* and make quarter turn.

Figure 126. As the working leg moves into *arabesque,* the supporting leg sinks into *fondu.*

(c) *Grands Fouettés en Tournant*

The swift *rotation* of the legs and half turn of the body at the height of the jump, rise or *relevé* in *grands fouettés* depends upon the impetus given by the working leg as it pushes into and out of the floor. This strong movement should be identical with that of a *grand battement devant* from first position *demi-plié*. But the height and accuracy of the jump, rise or *relevé* depends upon the pressure into and push out of the floor given by the other leg which first supports the weight of the body and then propels it into the air. It is a fraction of a second AFTER the upwards movement reaches its height that the body and working leg have to make the swift adjustments by a half turn and *rotation* of the leg in its socket in order to land correctly and be held firmly as the supporting toe, heel, knee and hip descend IN THAT ORDER, into *fondu*.

As in *rotation*, when moving *en dehors* the body must be seen to be erect before the half turn and *rotation* to finish in *arabesque* and when moving *en dedans*, the *arabesque* should be seen at the height of the jump, rise or *relevé* before the half turn and finish with the working leg held at 90° *devant*. The latter is one of of the most difficult movements to perform.

The *ports de bras* for *grands fouettés* can be varied. Nevertheless the arms should always help the body upwards, e.g. if the arms commence in second position with a preparation from *pointe tendue derrière*, as the working foot passes through first position the arms should fall to *bras bas* and with the *battement devant* and jump or rise, they should pass through first to fifth position at the height of the movement and open to second simultaneously with the turn and *rotation* of the leg. Or having reached first, open to *arabesque*, remembering that the new supporting hand should not grasp the barre until the hips and shoulders are square to their new front, otherwise the shoulders will be twisted. To help the upwards lift of the arms and body, there should be an intake of breath as the working leg passes through first to the *grand battement* and jump, rise or *relevé*. The breath is held during the turn and landing, and exhaled as the supporting knee moves into *fondu*. Another breath should be taken as the knee stretches upwards to ensure a firmly held pose.

XII. *Controlling the Spine in Grands Jetés en Avant and other Steps of Elevation*

Children should be taught early that the correct use of a strong, flexible spine will give each step of elevation its proper impetus and line. Later it is noted how the body must be inclined towards the direction travelled in *sissonnes* (p. 133); and how to co-ordinate it with the action of the legs to mark the difference between *assemblés en place* and *portés* (see p. 91.) The exercise for *grands fouettés* (see above) is easily repeated in the center either as adagio or allegro when it has been practised at the barre. It is also important to introduce *grands jetés en avant* at the barre so that children can appreciate how to direct their bodies through the air and distinguish between the romantic style *grand jeté* of *Giselle* which ascends upwards in a curve and downwards into an *arabesque*, and the modern style straight dart through the air of Lander's *Etudes* and the *grands jetés développés* of much Soviet choreography.

It is the romantic *grand jeté en avant* which is the most difficult to perform because of its need to soar upwards and then descend softly and calmly into *arabesque fondu*. The spine plays a most important part in this beautiful step and must be used to give that same upwards and slightly backwards stretch essential to any *arabesque* at the beginning of the spring into the air, thus directing the body and legs into the curved line required. Once the spine and leg are fully stretched, they must be held calm and still during the flight through the air and descend, still held, into *fondu*. In this way the *arabesque* itself can be said to have been projected through the air from one point to another.

The following exercise was taught by Fokine and created during his work on *Les Sylphides*. Not only is it an excellent introduction to this important step, but is also a very strengthening exercise for adagio where there has to be a slow transfer of weight from one pose to another.

EXERCISE 25. *GRANDS JETÉS EN AVANT* AT THE BARRE

Dance to four bars of grand waltz. Commence fifth position, right foot front. On anacrusis raise left foot to *petit retiré derrière*.

Bars
1. *Coupé devant* and *fondu* (figure 127).
2. Breathe in rising on left foot and stretching right leg forwards and upwards to its fullest extent (but not above 90°) simultaneously stretching spine upwards and very slightly backwards (figure 128).
3. Holding body still and slowly exhaling, follow the line of the raised leg downwards. At the moment when the toe reaches the floor, the right leg becomes the new supporting leg and descends gradually into *fondu*. At the same moment the toes of the hitherto supporting left leg leave the floor and rise into *arabesque* as the weight of the body is transferred forwards over the new supporting leg (figure 129).
4. Draw left foot into fifth *derrière* stretching legs and body erect and immediately raise right leg into *petit retiré devant*.
   Repeat, moving backwards:
   1. *Coupé derrière* and *fondu*.
   2. Breathe in, rising on right foot and stretching left leg backwards and upwards to its fullest extent (not above 90°), simultaneously stretching spine upwards and tilting the pelvis forwards to obtain an *arabesque* line.
   3. Holding body still and slowly exhaling, follow the line of the raised leg downwards. At that moment when the toes reach the floor the left leg becomes the new supporting leg and descends gradually into *fondu*. At the same moment the toes of the right leg must leave the floor and rise as the weight of the body is propelled backwards and transferred over to the new supporting leg.

4. Draw right foot into fifth *devant*, stretching legs and body erect. Immediately raise left leg into *petit retiré derrière*.

Repeat whole and then repeat on other side.

In other words when jumping *grands jetés en avant* in a romantic style, the body is propelled into a curve because the spine has been stretched upwards and slightly backwards to tilt the angle of the raised leg so that the impetus given by the spring (or rise) from the supporting leg must not only lift the body into the air, but must also be sufficient to propel the weight forwards over the leading foot before it reaches the floor. This transfer can only take place if the body and legs retain the same relationship reached when the initial stretching movement is at its fullest.

In the modern more athletic darted *grands jetés*, the impetus comes as much from the spring off the floor as from the preparatory *battement devant* when both legs stretch outwards and along simultaneously. In some cases the dancers then attempt to lift both legs higher (figure 130).

In the *grands jetés développés* the dancer springs into the air with the working leg in *retiré* (not very turned-out) and immediately stretches it forwards, occasionally arching the spine at the height of the jump.

But in neither of the above *grands jetés* does the spine have to give an extra stretch with the initial rise into the air. It is enough to keep it firm and still. And in neither of these two jumps is it possible to descend into *arabesque fondu*. If such is required, then the dancer must relax both the body and the raised leg as the supporting leg relaxes in *fondu*, and only after this, stretch into *arabesque*, the curving line not having been held during the leap.

Figure 130. Boy in *grand jeté*.

Figure 127. Coupé en fondu.

Figure 128. Open leg front and rise to *demi-pointe*. Stretch back.

Figure 129. Follow toe downwards to *fondu* and raise other leg to *arabesque*.

As a general rule it is not advisable to stretch children until they have developed some maturity of movement except by giving exercises in which they are using their own limbs as a lever to put extra pressure on one or another set of muscles to stretch them and, at the same time, strengthen the spine, as in the lunging exercise (see p. 98). However the introduction of *battements en cloche* can be a valuable exercise to loosen both legs and body provided that the pupil understands that no matter how high the working leg swings through from back to front and vice-versa, the supporting leg must remain absolutely perpendicular to the floor as well as firm and still. If it rocks to and fro the whole purpose of the exercise is lost for thigh and buttock muscles as well as those round pelvis and waist are being strained and not stretched.

When first teaching this movement the teacher must insist each child takes the correct stance in first position and then moves the working foot to *pointe tendue derrière*, the weight being held well over the supporting leg. From this position the child should be encouraged to swing the working leg directly through first to *pointe tendue devant* in such a way that the ankle and instep do most of the work and the heel is pushed firmly along the floor as it passes through thus stretching all the muscles inside the working leg if it is properly turned-out and the "gap" is maintained on both the working and supporting sides of the body, which remains erect and still.

As soon as this slow gliding movement to and fro is mastered, the working leg should be thrown up to 18°, the same care being taken to push the heel into the floor as it passes through first and to maintain the "gap" and erect body.

However, once the leg is thrown over 18°, first to 45° and then 90° or over, much greater care must be taken to keep the spine fully stretched and the supporting leg perpendicular to the floor and still. On no account should the pelvis be "rocked" (i.e. by the arching of the back at the waist) in order to throw the leg up at the back. Instead the weight of the body must be kept well forwards over the supporting leg, the rib-cage well lifted from the waist by the strong upwards pull of the stomach and inner costal muscles and an extra stretch upwards and backwards of the cervical spine. If this is done, the working leg will swing to and fro more freely in the hip socket and thus very little movement be seen in the upper half of the body.

Battements en cloche should not be mistaken for *battements balançoire*, although both originate from the same preparatory movement of swinging the leg from front to back. Whereas the value of *battements en cloche* is to loosen and stretch the legs whilst keeping the spine as strongly erect as possible, the purpose of *battements balançoire* is to make the spine more flexible at the same time as strengthening it and the pelvic muscles. Thus when the leg begins to swing through from back to front above 18° the body must stretch slightly backwards from the waist and as the legs swings through to the back, so the body "tilts" or "bows" forwards from the hinge into a true *arabesque* line. Thus, when the working leg swings above 90° at the back, the body will move equally forwards into *arabesque penché* and when it moves above 90° front, the body should balance equally backwards.

A valuable way of getting a child to "feel" the stretch of the muscles in buttocks, thighs and inside of the turned-out leg is to practise *battements en cloche* commencing in first position and swinging the working leg upwards into a well turned-out and open *attitude devant*, then pushing it downwards so that the heel with the fully stretched leg muscles rests momentarily and firmly in first position before swinging it upwards into an open *attitude derrière* as high as possible without in any way displacing the working leg or body.

Throughout all such exercises the arm should be held still in a well rounded second, the head either being held still, or inclined over the supporting leg when moving backwards and over the working leg when moving forwards in order to prevent tension across the shoulders and neck.

12

TRAINING FOR POINTE-WORK

THE two essentials to consider when placing girls *sur les pointes* for the first time are: firstly, to ensure that their metatarsal and longitudinal arches, ankles and knees are strong enough and that they can control and place their weight correctly over the centre line of balance. Secondly, to ensure that their shoes are suitable. The first item needs technical know-how and the second the ability to recognise a well-fitting shoe. Even if teachers do not fit them themselves, they should be able to explain why a shoe is not right.

KNOW-HOW AND KNOWLEDGE

Although the term know-how may seem a frivolous description of knowledge, a clear distinction must be made between the words as far as classical dance is concerned. Today many teachers are ex-male dancers only very few of whom have known how to rise, let alone dance, *sur les pointes*, whereas all women teachers will have had some practical knowledge. The male teacher can certainly acquire theoretical knowledge in general terms, but without experience of dancing *sur les pointes* he will have difficulties putting that into practice when faced with a class of girls each with a different shape and size of foot. Men have never felt that swift spring and stretch upwards into a *relevé* nor ever run soundlessly on the tips of their toes in *pas courus*. Nor have they experienced that search for the right size, shape and width of block, type of vamp and so on. Nor – having found the right shoe – tried to persuade the maker to supply others with exactly the same specifications.

Correctly-fitting pointe shoes are essential when a girl is first encouraged to rise correctly *sur les pointes*. They must fit snugly and NOT ALLOW FOR GROWTH. The toes should be able to spread only a little sideways and the tips just feel the block when standing with flat feet, the weight held correctly. But the metatarsal arch should be held firmly and comfortably within the toe-piece. The end of the outer leather sole does not come to the outer edge of the heel as in an ordinary shoe. This only happens when the girl is fully poised with outstretched foot on *pointe* because the back of the shoe should be deep enough to hold the shoe in place when the ribbons have been correctly stitched on. They must slope slightly forwards so that they can be wrapped round the ankle like a bandage and thus keep the heel-piece well rounded. Pointe shoes should always be moulded with the hands before wearing and worn at home before class so that the soles and blocks are a little more flexible, particularly under the instep and ball of the foot. The sole should be able to bend a little upwards and downwards, otherwise the feet cannot work properly when rising through the three points of balance (see figure 34).

TYPES OF FOOT

The ideal foot for pointe-work would be one in which four toes are of equal length. This is very rare and only encountered three times in my teaching career. These girls possessed wonderfully natural platforms on which to balance and this made pointe-work so easy they felt it was merely another item to practise daily, no matter how soft the shoes. Those with two or sometimes three toes of equal length usually find *pointes* easier than those where the big or second toe is longer than its neighbours. This type of foot presents problems, as do those with over-arched insteps. These may look beautiful but are usually weak because, when on *pointe*, the toes usually curl under, therefore the fore-foot and insteps are forced downwards and forwards from the ankle which is also weak. This means that the weight is incorrectly centred through the bones of the legs, and the muscles of the knees and thighs are strained. This affects the whole of the upper torso, particularly the shoulders and neck.

The average foot slopes downwards from the big to the little toe joints. Because of this it must always be remembered that when on *pointe* the leg is never so turned-out as it is when the foot is flat. Thus the first requisite in any *pointe* class is to ensure each girl knows exactly where the centre of balance lies in her own foot (see figures 2 and 18b). It is usually somewhere between the first and second and very occasionally third phalanges of the metatarsal arch. It rather depends on the length of the toes when on *demi-pointe*. This is the point where the girl feels a slight pressure just before the final rise, which must be taken straight upwards on to the tips of the toes, i.e. she rises through quarter, half and three-quarter *pointe* then makes a very slight spring on to the tips of the toes which replace the three-quarter *pointe*. (In some cases if the toes are short or the instep flat, the spring is taken from *demi-pointe*.) This tiny spring is minutely backwards and must be made to stretch both ankle and toes to their fullest extent downwards and outwards, so that the heel is not pulled backwards into the achilles tendon.

RISES THROUGH THE FEET

Before attempting pointe-work girls must spend much time strengthening both feet and ankles by practising rises through the three positions of the feet. These should be tried facing the barre with unturned-out legs rising and falling very slowly from four to eight times without bending the knees. The rises must be directly up and down, the girls feeling that the weight is always held forwards over the toes (figure 130). Then the feet are turned outwards into first position and the series repeated. These rises in first position are followed by a similar number of quick, relaxed *demi-pliés* and rises. The latter are only so high that the tips of the toes scarcely leave the floor, yet all the leg muscles are fully stretched and ready to hold the weight of the body up *sur les pointes*. These quick rises must be accompanied by the feeling that the body is being lifted away from the floor by the sheer power of the muscles within the thighs and pelvis as well as the feet. It is essential that the legs

Figure 130. Rise on *pointes* legs turned-in.

are directly under the body and do not spring forwards or backwards, as sometimes happens. Nor must the upper body and head move in any direction but up and down on the same line as it did when the legs were unturned-out. The girl should always feel that the heels and inside legs are kept together as long as possible by the strong inwards and outwards pull of the inner thigh muscles at the back of the legs, whilst the outer muscles are also being pulled upwards and the calf muscles downwards.

Each girl should feel she is pushing herself upwards from the feet and being set downwards from and to the same spot in an absolutely straight line by the strength of her feet and ankles. This is even more important when she opens them to second position and practises the same rises. The small second position should be used as this helps to strengthen the thigh muscles and the girl should then be able to feel how to use the strong outwards and round pull under the buttocks of all the muscles controlling turn-out.

With care it is never long before the rise to full *pointe* in first and second position can be tried and the HOLD at the height of the rise become stronger and longer before the heels are lowered through the same levels.

Figure 131. Step on to *pointe*, legs turned-in.

STEPPING ON TO POINTES

A second exercise for strengthening feet and ankles is to stand with legs unturned-out as above, facing the barre and proceeding as follows:

1. Lift the right leg into *retiré* directly in front of its own hip with the tip of the toe at the side of the supporting knee.

2. Step on to the right *pointe*, fully straightening the knee and simultaneously raising the left leg into *retiré*.

3–4. Hold this position momentarily then lower the left toe beside the right so that the weight is taken on both *pointes* before sinking on both feet through the proper levels (figures 131–2).

Figure 132. Step on to *pointe*, legs turned out.

(a) Posé to retiré devant

(b) Posé to retiré other foot. Note how far girls have travelled.

Figure 133. Pas de bourrée.

Once this exercise has been mastered it should be developed into *pas de bourrée dessus*, i.e. commencing in third or preferably fifth position, right foot *derrière, demi-plié.*

1. Step directly on to right *pointe* exactly behind the centre of the left foot, immediately raising the left knee into *retiré devant.*
2. Step slightly sideways into first position *sur les pointes*, transferring the weight and immediately raising the right knee into *retiré devant.*
3–4. Close *devant sur les pointes* before sinking into *demi-plié* through both feet.
   Repeat, picking up left foot.

It is best to practise *pas de bourrée* in this way first as it helps to maintain turn-out. Also when girls practise facing the mirror they are able to see how to control their hips and pelvis. The movements must be up and down only, with a very slight travel from side to side. Once mastered, instead of closing in fifth position, the girls should drop into *fondu* on the third step and pick up the back leg into *retiré*. In this way they will achieve the up, up, down rhythm typical of all *pas de bourrée* (figures 133a and 133b).

It is the direct upwards lift over and on to the supporting leg which must be mastered before stepping into a *posé*. This is best practised at the barre from fifth position and a brief *demi-plié*.

1. Move directly sideways by slightly raising the right leg fully stretched just off the floor and immediately step on to the right *pointe*, transferring weight and raising the left knee into *retiré derrière*.

2. Hold this position momentarily then *coupé*: i.e. drop the left foot into *fondu* directly behind the right leg which immediately stretches sideways ready to repeat the *posé*.

This *posé-coupé* should be repeated three times, the third closing in fifth position *derrière*, followed by a *battement tendu à la seconde* with the erstwhile supporting leg closing in fifth position *derrière*, ready to repeat to the left.

In both *posés* and *pas de bourrée* exercises the hands and ultimately only the finger-tips should rest on the top of the barre. As soon as balance is seen to be maintained in both exercises, they should be practised in the centre. It is very valuable gradually to increase the speed of the *pas de bourrée* as this helps to keep foot-work light and neat during the early stages of pointe-work. It is also valuable to practise *posés sur les pointes* moving *écarté* diagonally across the studio as a preparation for *posés pirouettes*. Similarly, use *posés en avant* from one foot to the other so that the girl feels the need directly to transfer weight over on to the supporting leg immediately she steps on *pointe*. Thus the step forwards must not be too big nor the *retiré* too high if the weight is to be carried upwards and forwards all the time. The movement should also be practised moving backwards, but at a later stage, as this requires much greater control and the correct use of the head and back.

RELEVÉS

The next strengthening exercise must be to master the various types of *relevés* and *échappés sur les pointes* on both feet. They must be practised facing and with both hands on the barre to a 3/4 time signature, which allows a *relevé* on the first beat, a hold in position on the second and a close in *demi-plié* on the third.

There are two ways to perform a *relevé* on both feet and these should be clearly understood. Both are equally valuable but have different uses. During the first stages it is essential that the very slight spring on to the tips of the toes from half or three-quarter *pointes* on both feet should find the tips coming minutely backwards to replace the metatarsal arch (i.e. those with short toes come from *demi-pointe*) or from the pads of the toes (i.e. those coming from three-quarter *pointe*). This means that the full stretch of the feet is reached when the legs are very slightly apart, so that when the feet are lowered into first position the heels are together again. Also it is essential that the weight is fully centred and held away from the waist. This means that all the muscles of the legs and torso must be absolutely firm and controlled. Only in this way can balance be maintained. The same very minute spring backwards must be practised in *relevés à la seconde*. These must be taken from a small second position, a similar small position to be used later when practising *relevés* in fourth opposite fifth position.

It is when dancing *relevés* in fifth position that the second form must be used. At the height of the *relevé* the insides of the legs should touch, particularly between the lower calf and ankle, so that the body and thus the weight is directly upwards through the centre line drawn between the fully pointed toes and the crown of the head. On no account must the big toes be pulled towards each other so that the big toe joints are pressed outwards and downwards. The exact placing of the feet in fifth position *sur les pointes* is all-important and arises from the preparatory *demi-plié*. In this, the front heel must not quite cover the back heel. It should come roughly as far as the cuticle of the big toe nail. (This is very important if the toes are short.) If it reaches too far across, the very slight spring upwards will find the legs too far apart to balance correctly. It is the close proximity of the inner legs when in fifth position that is going to be invaluable when *pas de bourrée suivis* or *courus* are practised later (figure 134).

Figure 134. Relevé in 5th. Not every girl has pulled her weight away from her feet and legs.

ÉCHAPPÉS

Échappés in second and fifth positions are a logical development from *relevés* on two feet. Once the open *relevés* in first and second positions and the closed ones in fifth have been mastered, the next steps are *échappés à la seconde* with a change of feet on each closing. They begin from a brief *demi-plié* in fifth position right foot front.
1. Spring with both feet apart rising on to full *pointe* in a small second position. Both legs must be fully stretched, the feet reaching the same height simultaneously.
2. Hold.
3. Spring both feet lightly together into fifth position *demi-plié*, left foot in front.

Figure 135. Échappé à la seconde. Note varying shapes
and sizes of feet and legs.

Repeat commencing left foot front and finishing right foot front. Repeat these
échappés from four to eight times and as soon as possible away from the barre,
opening the arms from *bras bas* to *demi-seconde* as this helps to keep the weight
central. If it is not, the hips may be twisted, or one leg not so strongly stretched as
the other. Both legs are equally responsible for holding the weight of the body
upwards and away from the floor (figure 135).

When repeating *échappés* from fifth to fifth position, much greater control is
needed as the legs should only open as far as first position *sur les pointes*, i.e. the heels,
when on full *pointe*, should only be far enough apart to allow the feet to pass easily
in front or behind each other before closing in a fifth position *demi-plié*. When
dancing these *relevés* in a series it is helpful to raise the arms from *bras bas* through
first to fifth and down to second position, as this circling of the arms helps to keep
the weight upwards and slightly forwards through the centre of the legs, ankles and
toes. It also prevents the shoulders pulling the torso backwards. These *échappés* in
fifth position are very valuable if practised in a quick tempo with a minimum *demi-plié* between each. They should later be attempted with no *demi-plié* at all.

Relevés échappés should also be practised opening from fifth position to a small
fourth and closing again in fourth as this is often necessary as a preparation for
pirouettes. It is useful to practise these *échappés* into fourth position alternately with
échappés à la seconde, changing feet. These are used to introduce a change of *épaulement*,
i.e. from a fifth position right foot front and a brief *demi-plié*.

1. *Échappé croisé* into fourth position, arms in third, close fifth.
2. *Échappé à la seconde de face* opening arms to *demi-seconde* and closing feet in fifth
   position left foot front, arms to first.
3. *Échappé croisé* into fourth position, arms in third and closing fifth, *demi-plié*, arms
   to first.
4. *Échappé à la seconde de face* as above, but closing the right foot front ready to start
   again.

This exercise helps the girl to understand how to make a slight spring and turn from one placing to another without losing control over her balance.

RELEVÉS ON ONE FOOT

It takes some time before girls are strong enough to perform a series of *relevés* on one foot, the other held in *retiré*, and much longer before they can attempt the *relevés retirés developpés*, so much a part of the ballerina's vocabulary, where she opens and closes the working leg at an angle of 90° as she sinks and rises on her supporting one. The *fondu* into *relevé* requires a keen sense of balance and strength in every muscle in that leg.

Simple *relevés* should first be practised *en place* at the barre before attempting to travel in any direction. They should be commenced in fifth position right foot front with a brief *demi-plié*.

1. *Relevé* and close in fifth position *demi-plié* to establish placing.
2. *Relevé* on left foot raising the right knee into *retiré*, with the toe level and at the side of the supporting knee.
3. Hold position momentarily.
4. Close right foot behind the left on full *pointe* and then lower the heels into fifth position *demi-plié*.

Repeat using the other foot. Then repeat, using *relevé retiré passé devant*.

In each of the above *relevés* the raised foot should return to fifth *sur les pointes* so that both feet lower the heels together into *demi-plié*. This is to ensure the weight is always fully centred.

Once this simple exercise has been mastered, the amount of *relevés* on one foot only should be increased. Only when both legs and feet seem strong enough should girls attempt to open the raised working leg out to the front, back or side during the *relevé* before closing it appropriately into *retiré* on the *fondu*, i.e to the centre of the front, back or side of the calf or knee. The height of the *retiré* will depend on the height required by the finished pose. The upper leg should remain at that same height during the opening and closing as this helps to keep the weight centered.

SISSONNES FERMÉES DESSUS-DESSOUS

It is when the above *relevés* have to be travelled on one foot that the girl has to be encouraged to give a slight spring into the appropriate direction by practising *sissonnes fermées dessus-dessous* to prevent problems arising. Commence in fifth position right foot front and a brief *demi-plié*.

1. Spring sideways to the right on right full *pointe*, simultaneously opening and stretching the left leg *à la seconde* at 45°.
2. The right supporting leg now sinks into *fondu* before the left closes into fifth position *devant* in *demi-plié*.

Repeat with the same foot, but the left will close fifth *derrière*. Continue repeating this at least four times before repeating to the other side.

(a) Devant

(b) Écarté

(c) Derrière

Figure 136. First attempts at *sissonnes sur les pointes.* Some girls are already showing a proper sense of line.

129

As in all pointe-work it is essential that the weight of the body is transferred directly over and on to the supporting leg as in all the other *relevés* and *posés*. For this reason the hips must be strictly controlled, the weight lifted away from the waist and both legs bending and stretching equally and strongly at all times (figures 136a, b and c).

RELEVÉS AND PIROUETTES

Once these *sissonnes* have been mastered moving *en croix*, then *relevés retirés developpés* on one leg only must be practised, moving in every direction. Similarly, once *relevés retirés passés* from fifth to fifth or fourth positions are mastered, single *pirouettes en dehors* should be attempted. These are easier to accomplish, beginning from a *relevé retiré passé* from fifth to a small fourth *demi-plié* as the preparation for the *pirouette*, which should finish fifth *demi-plié derrière* ready to repeat from the other side. *Pirouettes en dedans sur les pointes* are also best taken from a small fourth position and without a *fouetté* preparation. These should finish fifth *devant*. Thus if practised in a series commencing with a *relevé retiré passé derrière* (as in those moving *en dehors* above) they always repeat with the same foot. The difficulty for beginners using the *fouetté* preparation is usually lack of strength and stability, as well as the ability to time the movement so that the rise to *pointe* occurs simultaneously with the whip of the other leg from *à la seconde* to *retiré* and turn. The girl is apt to lose control over the supporting hip and leg in her anxiety to maintain turn-out.

13

NOTES ON THE DIFFERENCES BETWEEN
CERTAIN STEPS

CHILDREN should be taught early in training that certain steps need to be accurately performed if their particular quality is to be clearly defined. Sometimes it is a simple matter of a slight difference in movement, as between a *battement tendu* and a *battement glissé*, or between a rise and a *relevé* (see p. 39). But sometimes the exact action and accent must be changed. The following are those steps most frequently confused.

I. JUMPS IN FIRST POSITION, SOUBRESAUTS, CHANGEMENTS DE PIEDS, CHANGEMENTS BATTUS AND ENTRECHATS QUATRE

In each case the jump upwards proceeds from a *demi-plié* and continues until the legs are stretched with toes fully pointed at the height of the jump, the feet returning to the closed position. But in each case the action is slightly different.

(a) *Jumps in first position*. The feet never change their relationship, i.e. from the *demi-plié* in first position the jump must be seen to rise through the legs until the toes are fully pointed with the heels closed together at the height of the jump (figure 19).

(b) *Soubresauts*. Whether performed *en place* or travelled from *demi-plié* in fifth position, the jump must be seen to rise through the legs until the toes are fully pointed with the legs still held together at the height of the jump (figure 38).

(c) *Changements*. From *demi-plié* in fifth position, the jump must be seen to rise through the legs, which gradually open so that the heels and fully pointed toes are seen to be slightly apart at the height of the jump. Their relationship then changes before the toes reach the floor on the descent.

(d) *Changements Battus*. From *demi-plié* in fifth position, the jump must be seen to rise through the legs which gradually open as in *changements*. But at the height of the jump, the legs are drawn together and beaten in the SAME RELATIONSHIP with which they began the jump, and only after this beaten movement do they re-open to change their relationship during the descent into fifth position.

Changements Battus are sometimes called *Royale*, supposedly after the efforts of King Louis XIV to dance when he got too fat; but the correct *Royale* commences and finishes in a small second position, the beat occurring as the fully pointed feet are drawn together in the air, before re-opening into small second position (Old French school).

(e) *Entrechat Quatre*. From *demi-plié* in fifth position the jump must be seen to rise through the legs. At the height of the jump they are apart with fully pointed toes, then drawn together and beaten AFTER HAVING CHANGED THEIR RELATIONSHIP. After this beat, they are re-opened and descend into fifth position in the same relationship with which they began the descent.

2. TEMPS LEVÉ, SISSONNE SIMPLE (OR ORDINAIRE). ASSEMBLÉ SIMPLE (OR PETIT ASSEMBLÉ) AND RETIRÉS PASSES SAUTES

(a) *Temps Levé* is any jump upwards from one foot commencing *fondu* and landing on that same foot, with the working leg held in the same pose with which the spring began. The jump must be seen to rise from the *fondu* until the leg is stretched with fully pointed toe, which should be at least two inches from the floor.

(b) *Sissonne Simple (or ordinaire)*. From a *demi-plié* in third position or fifth position the jump must be seen to rise through both legs until they are stretched with toes fully pointed then – when the toes are about to touch the floor as the feet descend into third or fifth position, one foot is snatched up the front or back of the supporting leg to *petit retiré*, or as high as the following movement requires.

(c) *Assemblé Simple (or petit assemblé)*. The jump commences with the working foot already held in a low or high *retiré*. From *fondu* the supporting leg springs up until stretched with fully pointed toe. At the height of the jump the working foot is stretched downwards so that both feet descend together into fifth *demi-plié*.

(d) *Retiré Sauté, Retiré Passé Sauté*. These commence from fifth position but as the dancer springs upwards, the working toe is snatched upwards so that the fully pointed working toe reaches the side of the other knee at the height of the jump (see p. 107). The working leg then descends to its original starting position, or changes its relationship to the supporting leg (i.e. if a *passé* movement is required) and arrives at the position together with the supporting leg.

3. ASSEMBLÉS AND SISSONNES FERMÉES

Although the different qualities of these steps should be quite evident, beginners make mistakes in their efforts to distinguish one from the other.

(a) The basic *assemblé en place* begins with a firm *demi-plié* in fifth position, the working foot is pushed outwards along the floor to side, front or back until the leg is fully extended with toe pointed. At the moment when the working toe is carried slightly upwards by the impetus given from ankle to instep, the supporting leg springs upwards until it too is fully stretched. At the height of the jump the extended leg is brought back to the supporting leg and both descend together into fifth position (see p. 91).

(b) *Assemblé Porté*. This commences as *assemblé en place* but the working foot is given greater impetus to travel so that it is pushed further upwards to any angle between 45° and 90° and, as it leaves the floor, the supporting leg requires a more powerful spring upwards and sideways, forwards or backwards to the point indicated by the extended working leg. At the height of the jump the legs join and descend together into fifth *demi-plié* at the new point.

N.B. The strong push into and out of the floor given by the working foot should be strong enough for the supporting leg to travel upwards and along as it leaves the floor. However the working leg must not be dropped backwards. It must be seen to be drawn downwards as the jumping leg travels, NOT MERELY AS IT RISES from the floor with the spring (see p. 91).

(c) *Sissonnes Fermées.* From a *demi-plié* in fifth position both legs are joined and spring upwards in the appropriate direction until both legs are stretched with toes fully pointed and have propelled the body sideways, forwards or backwards in the air. At the height of the jump the legs part, that nearest the floor (i.e. in the direction travelled) then descends through toe, ankle and knee to *fondu*, and is followed by the other leg, which glides along the floor to close in fifth position as the supporting leg straightens. This movement can only be stabilised if the descent and closing of the second leg is strongly controlled and co-ordinated with the straightening of the supporting leg.

If done in a series, then the second leg must be even more strongly controlled to glide into fifth position *demi-plié*, and the weight of the body more strongly held over the supporting leg as it descends into *fondu*. Moreover the body must be held still and slightly inclined towards the direction in which the *sissonne* travels.

(d) *Sissonnes Ouvertes.* Commence as above, but when the supporting leg descends *fondu*, the other must be held in the appropriate pose. This means that the weight of the body must always be held very firmly over the supporting leg. Careful attention should be paid to the transfer of weight from the two feet of the preparatory position to the final pose over the supporting leg in *fondu*, and held as this knee straightens.

4. ASSEMBLÉS BATTUS AND BRISÉS

There is very little difference to be made between these two steps. In the Russian school the *assemblé battu* never travels, but the *brisé* does. In *assemblés battus* the working foot comes into the supporting foot before the beat; in *brisés* the supporting foot is taken outwards to the extended foot before beating. The beat is performed at some angle to the body in order to give line to the direction travelled.

5. DEMI-CONTRETEMPS AND FAILLI

The difference between these two steps should always be preserved as the former is usually used as a preparatory step for a movement covering space and/or height, whilst the latter, in its original form, was used as a preparatory step during *petit* or *grand batterie*. In some schools this has now become similar to a *temps de poisson*, but does not always show the upwards and slightly curved stretch of the spine needed in this beautiful step.

(a) *Demi-contretemps.* This should commence from an open position. If not, the working leg should be lifted lightly from the floor into a low *attitude* on an ancrusis or half beat before the supporting leg springs lightly upwards and along the line of dance on the beat of the music. (Thus retaining the slightly syncopated movement in the original use of this step, which means "against time"). The working foot then passes through first to fourth position with a firm transfer of weight forwards on to the new leading leg held in a strong *fondu*, the other posed in *pointe tendue derrière* (see p. 84).

(b) *Failli* (meaning "about to fall over") commences in fifth *demi-plié*. Both feet then spring upwards and forwards simultaneously with the body stretched slightly upwards. The movement should not be too high. The foot nearest the floor descends into a strong *fondu* so that the weight is firmly fixed over that leg before the other descends and passes through first to a small fourth *en avant*, during which the weight is transferred equally over both feet. The size of the final position will depend upon what is to follow.

(c) *Contretemps*. A *demi-contretemps* should not be confused with a full *contretemps* as it is danced today. The *contretemps* is a twentieth-century *enchâinement*.

14

FURTHER NOTES

1. NOTES ON STRENGTHENING THE SPINE DURING PORTS DE BRAS

CHILDREN are often told to keep their shoulders still during *ports de bras*, but if they breathe correctly this is impossible. The very act of moving the arms entails the use of the accessory respiratory muscles because they are part of the shoulder girdle (see p. 63), therefore every *ports de bras* should be co-ordinated with correct breathing. Moreover if all *ports de bras* and breathing are phrased musically the child is helped to space the movements and give an altogether more flowing quality to the lines made. These lines drawn through the air depend primarily on preserving the relationship between arms, shoulders, torso and head so that the patterns made are part of the total line of any step or pose.

The rules for the arm movements in classical dance are very simple, but too often forgotten. They are worth repeating:

1. The arms are always rounded except in *arabesque*, the palm of the hand and the inside of the elbow facing the same plane.

2. At all times both boy and girl should be able to turn their heads sideways when the arms are in second and open third or fourth and fifth position and glance down the back of their elbows.

3. The arms always slope slightly downwards from the shoulders when they are in first or second position, the fingertips being on a level with the diaphragm.

4. The fingertips never touch those of the other hand when the arms are in *bras bas*, first or fifth position. They are always two or four inches apart, according to the length of the arm and the sex of the dancer.

5. The arms and hands never touch the body in *bras bas* or in any other position (i.e. in the classroom).

6. Neither arm must cross the central line of the body. Nor should the wrists cross each other, except when dancing in romantic style where certain conventional poses are used (see also p. 78).

7. The arms and hands should always "feel" the pressure of the air as they are drawn inwards and outwards or upwards and downwards, just as the child should always "feel" that the rib-cage is pushing outwards and relaxing inwards when breathing, because there is pressure of air round the torso. This pressure is never diminished because the arms, if correctly held, offer no protection.

It is important always to bear these rules in mind particularly when practising *ports de bras* involving some body movement when all too often the arms do not retain their correct relationship to the shoulders and spine. This upsets the balance of body and legs, and occurs frequently when the child bends forwards and circles the arms from one side to the other, e.g. from an open fourth with the right arm up to an open fourth with the left arm up. This circling can be done in several ways (see below). But first the child should understand there are four ways of bending forwards.

1. The child keeps the spine absolutely still and "tilts" forwards from the "hinge" (figures 13, 14).

2. The child can gradually roll the spine downwards. Begin by stretching the head upwards before "feeling" it roll downwards, thus stretching the cervical before curving the rest of the spine until the body hangs fully relaxed as low as possible (figures 74, 75).

3. With arms in second, feet in first, third or fifth position, the child breathes in stretching upwards with a slight lift of the head and begins to "tilt" the pelvis forwards, then relaxes the head and rib-cage, graciously "bowing" and continues to control the movement of the body downwards, at the same time lowering the arms until the hands could pick something from the floor. (If they are correctly placed they are in first position with the body bent forwards.) From thence the body is stretched directly upwards and re-assumes its correct stance (figures 74–76).

This third forwards bend is the most frequently used on the stage as it is part of *grand reverence* (see p. 141). It is also used when circling the arms in the following *ports de bras*.

4. There is yet another version of the forwards bend which is of the greatest value in stretching and strengthening the spine. With arms in second and feet in first, third or fifth position, the child breathes in, stretching upwards before "tilting the pelvis" forwards as in the first version, until the body lies parallel with the floor, (i.e. 90° to the body). At this point relax the body and arms and continue downwards as far as possible. Then begin to raise body and arms until the same point is reached at which relaxation took place. At this point, stretch the body straight forwards (i.e. till it is again parallel to the floor) and move arms into fifth position. Then continue upwards with a perfectly straight spine from the "hinge" upwards.

1. *The Simplest Form*

Dance to four bars of slow waltz. Commence fifth *de face*, left foot front, arms in open fourth, right arm up.

Bars

1. Breathe in, increasing the "Gap" and still holding position bend forwards as far as possible, keeping the arms still.
2. Exhale, keeping body still and change arms, maintaining them the same distance apart so that by the third beat their relationship is reversed.
3. Breathe in and recover erect stance, the body and head alone making the movement.
4. Exhale and *battement tendu* side to change feet.
   Repeat on other side (figures 137–141).

Figure 137. Stand in fifth position, arms open fourth, opposite arm up to let in front.

Figure 138. Begin to bend forwards.

Figure 139. Relax and lower body.

Figure 140. Change arms.

Figure 141. Straighten and gaze into hand.

N.B. Care must be taken to prevent the arms swinging behind the shoulders at any time during this movement. The legs are held perpendicular to the floor, the weight is firmly centred over both feet. The head and spine stretch upwards with the intake of breath and when the descending body lies roughly parallel to the floor, the head and rib-cage slightly relax and remain so until the body reaches the same point when it ascends. At this point the head takes control and stretches upwards to lead the body to the correct position.

2. *A more Difficult Version*

This demands that all the details of the above note must be followed, but the body from the waist upwards now plays a part to increase the semi-circular line of the *ports de bras*.

Dance to eight bars of smooth waltz and commence as above.

Bars

1–2. Breathe in stretching upwards to increase the "gap" and turn the body from the waist as far as possible to the left, then bend forwards as far as possible until the right arm in fifth, is roughly midway between front and side.

3–4. Exhale while circling the body to the right, keeping it at the same level and changing the arms as before. The body should reach as far to the right as it was to the left. The left arm in fifth position is now roughly midway between front and side.

5–6. Breathe in, turning the body to face front as it ascends, and recover upright position.

7–8. *Battement tendu* side to change feet and repeat on other side.

3. *A Difficult Version*

This should only be attempted when students can control all the muscles maintaining the "gap". It should be practised first at the barre and danced to eight bars of slow waltz. Commence fifth position, right foot front, left hand on barre, right arm in fifth position.

Bars

1–2. Breathe in, and holding right arm still, stretch upwards then bend sideways to the barre (figure 73).

3–4. Exhale and stretch body forwards trying to hold left shoulder at the same level as the body is drawn more downwards and is circled and stretched forwards. When it is half-way round, it should lie roughly parallel to the floor, the upper half slightly relaxed and right arm directly in front, (i.e. it does not move from fifth position during the circling).

5–6. Breathe in and out and continue circling until the body is bent sideways to the right and the right arm lowered to second position (not beyond). The head begins to stretch and slightly to incline to the right as it leads the movement round.

7–8. Breathe in, circling and stretching the body backwards by stretching the spine and leading the movement with the head. At the same time the right arm moves from second to fifth position. This is done with a turn of the wrist to bring the palm of the hand upwards so that when the spine is curved directly backwards the hand is again in fifth position. Continue circling until the body returns to the side. Straighten and correct stance.

This *ports de bras* requires an absolutely controlled head which LEADS the movement and arms which NEVER move behind the shoulder. Care must also be taken not to move the elbow at the barre. Do not allow it to twist upwards when the body circles forwards and then away from the barre to the other side.

The exercise is also valuable when practised in fifth position on *demi-pointe*, which not only helps to control and stretch all the leg muscles from the ball of the foot to the waist and thus keeps the legs firmly perpendicular. It also helps to strengthen and make more flexible all the muscles controlling the various parts of the spine, as well as encouraging its three curves to act correctly as shock absorbers (see p. 60).

All these exercises should be practised without pauses. A pause can only cause tension in one or another part of the body and thus distort the line, or upset the balance.

2. FURTHER NOTES ON PIROUETTES

Every *pirouette* and every balancing exercise should finish firmly on the supporting leg before the working foot moves from its position to be held in some pose, or descends to the final position. Only this gives strength and stability to the dancer moving from one step to another, particularly when moving from a *pirouette* into another step or a pose without placing the working foot on the floor. The girl in particular should remember that in the same way as she gives a very slight spring on to a full *pointe*, she must give an equally very slight spring off her *pointe* to bring her heel back to the floor before bending her supporting knee into *fondu* or both legs into *demi-plié*. Similarly the boy must lower the supporting heel before moving into *fondu* or *demi-plié*. In both cases it is essential to keep the weight firmly centred when lowering the heel of the supporting leg. Thus the instep of the girl's foot should be centred over the spot on which she turned or poised on full *pointe*, whilst the ball of the boy's foot remains over that spot. It is for this reason that the boy is more frequently expected to finish his *pirouettes* in some position where he pauses on two feet, or more quickly unfolds his working leg into some pose.

3. THE ORDER OF BARRE-WORK

The order in which exercises are given at the barre is very important as the work is designed to educate the body in proper sequence so that by the time centre work is reached, the child is warm and all the muscles respond easily and correctly. It is essential to begin with *demi-* and full *pliés*, the weight of the body centred firmly over both feet so that the pressure of weight helps to equalise the relaxing and stretching movements in the muscles of both legs, thighs, hips and pelvic girdle. *Pliés* should be followed by those stretching one leg after the other from hip to toe with a slow, strongly controlled but gentle action. *Battements tendus, glissés* (or *jetés*, i.e. over 30°) are ideal for this purpose as the feet and ankles are warmed by the friction made along the floor.

Ronds de jambe à terre should not be attempted until the legs are thoroughly warm as the effort of turning outwards and moving regularly from the hip-joints can be dangerous if the muscles in the lower half of the body have not been stretched a little and are cold. Many teachers prefer to use *grands battements* after *ronds à terre*, feeling that such exercises are a great help in loosening the legs to give height to the sustained efforts to follow in *battements fondus, grands ronds de jambe* and other adage. Others prefer to leave *grands battements* until the end of barre and use these instead of *battements en cloche* or *balançoire*.

But whichever order used, the teacher should always remember that barre work should proceed allowing the smaller and more sustained movements to be practised before those at 90° and faster, as well as those designed specially for loosening the limbs and body.

After leaving the barre, the same kind of order should prevail during centre work and as stated above, several exercises should be set which help the children to understand how barre work is only part of centre-work and its theories continue onwards into the adage and steps across the room.

The class should always finish with a *grand reverence*, the children coming forwards with a true classical walk before they bow. This walk has to be cultivated and must be carefully practised.

4. THE CLASSICAL WALK

Commence *de face* standing on right foot, left *pointe tendue derrière*, arms *bras bas*. Dance to slow 4/4, a sarabande, a pavane, polonaise, or slow waltz. Vary the time signature, but always dance very slowly and grandly. The following is timed to a sarabande.

Bars

1. Bending left knee slightly and retaining turn-out, pass fully pointed left foot past right (toe is roughly on level with right ankle), place left toe and then heel on floor a pace in front of right so that it falls into fourth opposite first position (but not too turned-out). At same time raise left arm through first and open to second position watching hand, then raising head to audience. The moment the left heel touches the floor, transfer weight forwards and begin bending right knee ready to step forwards on:

2. Repeat above using right foot and right arm.

3–4. Or as many bars as wished continue forwards. Having reached desired place and with weight on left foot perform *grand reverence*.

Figure 142. Step on to right foot opening right arm, etc.

Figure 143. Bring left foot behind right, lifting left hand, etc.

Bars
1. Step to right on right, and raise left *pointe tendue* side moving right arm into first position a little closer to body than usual, before opening arm broadly to second position glancing first at hand and then raising head and glancing round from centre to audience on right as left foot is drawn back and rests just behind right (toe pointed and resting on ground).
2. Repeat above movement to left being careful to glance at audience from centre to audience on left.

3. Step again to right slightly lifting arms and left foot *pointe tendue* side.
4. Draw left foot behind right and step back on it, dropping both arms to *bras bas* and bow deeply forwards lowering head.
5. Transfer weight fully on to left foot and stretch right *pointe tendue devant*, straightening head and body whilst re-opening arms into the widest possible second position as if to give one's thanks fully to the audience.
6–7–8. Hold this position (figure 145).

Figure 144. Step back on to left foot inclining body, etc.

Figure 145. Hold this position.